Reflections Worth Remembering

God

Faith

Family

Country

Dr. Roy W. Harris

Copyright 2017

By

Dr. Roy W. Harris

ISBN: 978-1-947759-01-5

Soft cover

All rights reserved.

No part of this book may be reproduced or transmitted in any form or by any means, electronic or mechanical, including photocopying, recording, or by any information storage and retrieval system, without permission in writing from the copyright owner.

This book was printed in the United States of America.

To order additional copies of this book, contact:

Dr. Roy W. Harris

roy@royharris.info

Order Online

@

www.amazon.com

Special Recognition

Special thanks to the organizations and individuals listed below who published articles written by me and a variety of other information pertaining to me and the ministries I've had the privilege of serving.

Contact Magazine (Former Magazine of The National Association of Free Will Baptists) - Dr. Jack Williams (deceased)

Free Will Baptist Bible College Bulletin (Now Welch College) – Burt Tippett (deceased)

ONE Magazine (Magazine of the National Association of Free Will Baptists) - Eric Thomsen

Wilson Living Magazine (Serving several counties in Middle Tennessee) Angel Kane & Becky Andrews

The Michigan Menorah (Michigan Free Will Baptist State Paper) – Gene Norris

The Arkansas Vision (Arkansas Free Will Baptist State Paper) Tim Campbell

The California Voice (California Free Will Baptist State Paper) – Dr. Millard Sasser

The Ohio Ambassador (Ohio Free Will Baptist State Paper) Edwin Hayes

The Mississippi Messenger (Mississippi Free Will Baptist State Paper) Dennis Kizzire

The Tennessee Echo (Tennessee Free Will Baptist State Paper) – Glenn Poston

The Florida Coordinator (Florida Free Will Baptist State Paper) - Reverend Randy Bryant, CMP

The Donelson Dispatch (Monthly Paper for the Donelson Fellowship) – Dr. Robert Morgan

USA Today (United States National Publication) Christopher Jones

Contents

INTRODUCTION

CHRISTIAN PRINCIPLES
Miracle in Chicago - 26
Where was God Last Friday? - 31
For the Love of the Game - 37
Why Tithe? - 43
Cicada Time in Tennessee - 49
Kindergarten Forgiveness - 54
The Verdict - 60
Everyday Labor - 66

UNITED STATES of AMERICA
America an Exceptional Nation - 70
The Repeal of Don't Ask – Don't Tell - 75
Same Sex Marriage – An Oxymoron - 81
The Leader of the Pack - 87
America The Great - 91
What Cost America - 97
Christian-a-Phobia - 101
How Should I Vote? - 107
How Shall We Then Live? - 113

FAMILY
A Caregiver's Blind Date - 119
The Greatest of These – Love - 123
Living Together - Not Married - 127
Married or Soon To Be - 134

How to Be Married - 139
Something About Moms - 144
Calling Faithful Men - 149
The Caregiver Checklist - 159

LEADERSHIP

Heard The News? - 164
CHRITICISM – Who Needs It? – 171
What is Your Boss Really Thinking? 177
COMMON SENSE LEADERSHIP – Q & A - 181
Diamond In The Rough - 187
The Interim Pastor - 193
It's Just Good Business - 202

HEALTH & HAPPINESS

What's It Worth - 211
Thank You Very Much - 217
Keeping It Together - 223
Surviving The Lonely Holidays - 228
Congratulations On Your Anniversary - 233
Eventide - 237
Vacation Time - 242
The End of Summer - 247
Living Beyond Grief - 251
Tag, You're It - 259
Out of Africa - 263

BOOKS IN PRINT

Caring for the Caregiver

Common Sense LEADERSHIP

Family Common Sense

Mentoring with Common Sense

Ministering in East Africa

ONGOZA Kwa UAMINIFU (Swahili)

Common Sense FAMILIES

KUSAIDIA KWA FAMILIA (Swahili)

Lead With Confidence

MALEZI YALIYO NA KIZIA KJEMA (Swahili)

When Angels Rejoice

Malaika Wanaposhiangilia (Swahili)

Living Beyond Grief

Dr. Roy W. Harris – Doctoral Dissertation

Care for Caregivers

(Reprint of Caring for the Caregiver)

Introduction

I will celebrate my 65th birthday this Saturday August 5, 2017. It's hard to believe how fast life passes. From time to time it is good for one to reflect on the past and remember things that may have been forgotten.

My passion for writing began when I at Washington Elementary School in Anderson, Indiana in the fifth grade. I made a wire sculpture of a little boy on one knee with his head in his hands. I then wrote a story related to the sculpture titled: *I was there at Hiroshima*. My teacher submitted the sculpture and story to a citywide competition of all fifth graders and I was for fortunate enough to win first place.

She presented the award to me and made me feel special. I cannot remember her exact words but she told me that I had a gift. *You feel things deeply and you have the unique ability at a young age of putting them on paper* she said. I never forgot that day and what she said. I continued writing during my two-years in the U.S. Army during the Viet Nam War and the years that followed.

I grew up, finished high school, earned Bachelor of Arts and Master of Ministry degrees from Welch College and a Doctor of Philosophy degree from Trinity Theological Seminary.

This book, **Reflections Worth Remembering,** is a collection of my articles that have been published in several local, statewide and national publications over the last 25 years. I selected a variety of articles addressing issues facing our nation, help for marriages and family, recognition of those who are important to us, our personal heath and application of Biblical principles.

The book can be great resource for insight into issues facing our nation, sermon or teaching illustrations, or just relaxing reading about everyday life. The articles represent many hours of thought, prayer and hard work.

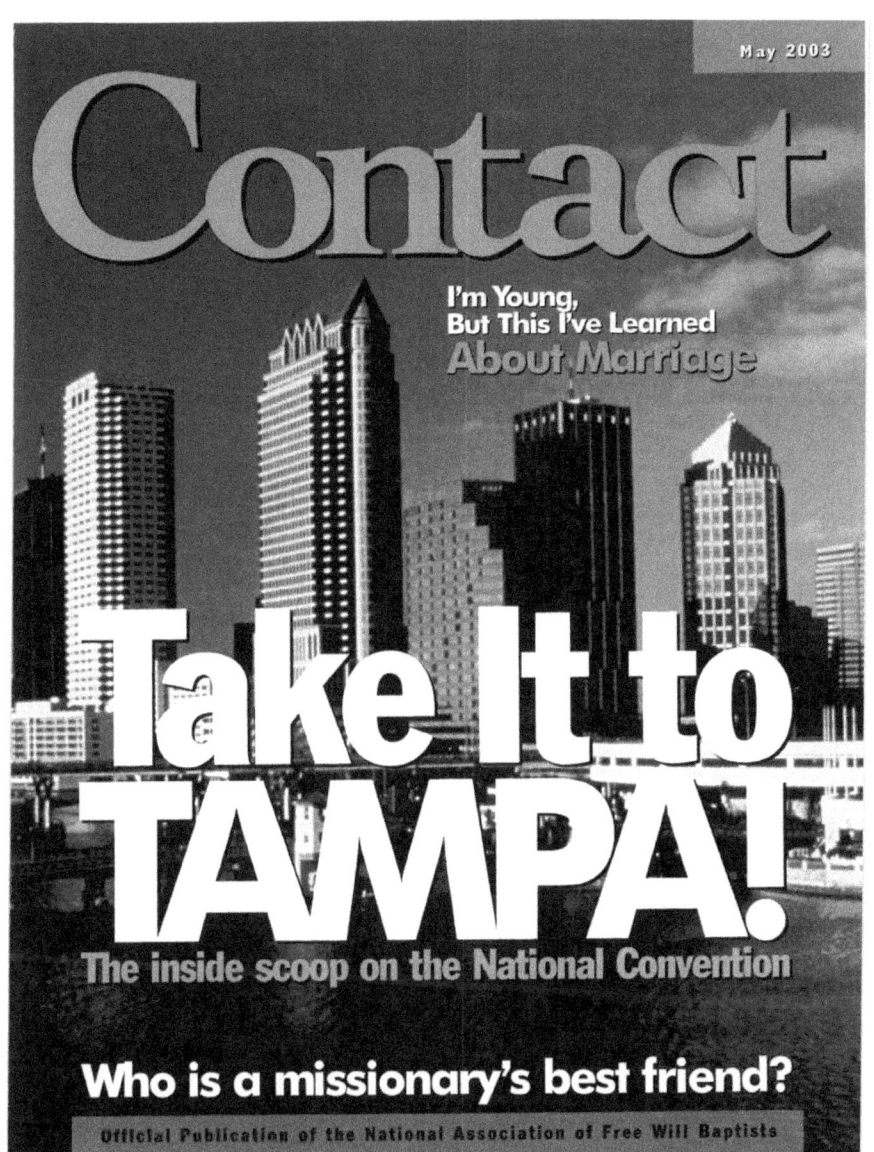

The Michigan Free Will Baptist
Menorah

April — A Monthly Publication of the Michigan State Association of Free Will Baptists — **2013**

Living Together – Not Married

Later today I will counsel with my second couple this week in preparation for their upcoming wedding. This reminded me of something I've wanted to do for some time; address the question of why marriage is important. I do not claim to have all the answers but I do speak as one who has experienced the wonderful joy of being married for a total of 38 years.

Our modern American culture has seemingly declared war on the oldest institution in the history of the world, marriage. It has sought to diminish the importance of marriage and relegate it to the dark closet of the old fashioned and declared it to be out of step with the times. Why address this? According to Michael McManus' book *Marriage Savers*, the problem has become epidemic. The number of couples living together outside of marriage has increased by 1200% since 1960.

There are problems when marriage is not valued.

I've sat in living rooms of couples who were living together while unmarried and heard them say things like; *we don't need a piece of paper to commit to one another for life*. Another statement; *we aren't hurting anyone or it's our business and nobody else's*. A culture which embraces this approach on face value without proof simply has not looked at the facts. *Eight out of ten couples* that live together before marriage will break up either before they marry or at some point after they marry. Couples who live together before marriage and eventually do get married are *50% more likely to divorce* than those who do not. *Only 12%* of couples who begin their relationship with cohabitation end up with a marriage that will last for *10 years*.

What about the statement; *it's nobody else's business and we aren't hurting anyone anyway*? Well, I would beg to disagree! It is….. our business because cohabitation does hurt others. Again the statistics bear this out. Children living in homes where couples are unmarried are *five times* more likely to grow up in *poverty* than those with married parents. These children are *twenty-two times* more likely to be *arrested* and end up *incarcerated*. These children are *three times* more likely to be *expelled* from school and *three times* more likely to end up in *teenage pregnancies*. These children are *ten times* more likely to be *sexually abused* by a stepparent than those growing up in homes with married parents. This lifestyle does impact the lives of others and it should be a concern to all of us. Divorce, child abuse, teenage pregnancy, high school drop outs and career criminals are a few problems that have already arisen from a culture that has sought to diminish the value and importance of marriage.

God has a planned relationship for society.

Reading and following directions usually will provide a better outcome than simply taking all the pieces and trying to make them work with no plan. God supplies the directions on how a society can survive and thrive. He began his instructions with the first institution he created and blessed. God created Adam and helped him understand that he was alone and needed someone to complete and enhance his life (Genesis 2). God reached next to Adam's heart and took a rib and created Eve. He brought her to Adam and blessed their newly established relationship. Have you ever thought about why so many people want church weddings? I believe a key reason is that they want God's blessing on their new life together. God creates men and women to complement each other. They need each other and supply those things which are necessary to find happiness and contentment. God established the paradigm for mankind. A man and a

OHIO AMBASSADOR

Volume 53 Number 1   January-February 2013

"The Voice of Ohio Free Will Baptists Proclaiming The Words of Christ to a Lost World"

Are You Bringing Vegetables to God?

New Year's Issue

Are you bringing vegetables to God? In Genesis, it records two men bringing their gifts to the Lord. One was accepted and one rejected. *"And in process of time it came to pass, that Cain brought of the fruit of the ground an offering unto the Lord. And Abel, he also brought of the firstlings of his flock and of the fat thereof. And the Lord had respect unto Abel and to his offering: But unto Cain and to his offering he had not respect.* (Genesis 4:3-5) The writer of Hebrews sheds some insight on why. *"By faith Abel offered unto God a more excellent sacrifice than Cain, by which he obtained witness that he was righteous, God testifying of his gifts: and by it he being dead yet speaketh."* (Hebrews 11:4)

Abel brings a sacrifice to God that is approved. His brother Cain brings an offering that is rejected.

Does this seem fair? After all Cain was a tiller of the ground and vegetables was what he raised. Abel, being a keeper of the sheep brought what he had raised. And in no place IN the previous three chapters does God give instructions as to the type of sacrifice He expected you may say.

In Genesis 3:23 the instructions were given as to the type of offering God will accept. The instructions were given by inference. (Inference is the act or process of deriving logical conclusions from premises known or assumed to be true.) The best way to teach and instruct is by example and God had given the example when innocent blood was shed to cover the nakedness brought about by the sins committed by Adam and Eve in the garden of Eden. Also we can all rest assured that Cain and Abel had been told about the innocent animals losing their lives for the benefit of their parents.

With this knowledge we conclude that these men each knew what type sacrifice God requires.

What thoughts went through the minds and hearts of Cain and Abel we aren't told but obviously, Abel had in his heart to give unto God what was expected to be given. God wants a blood sacrifice then I must present to Him a blood sacrifice. This tells the world that what the Lord requires must be met precisely.

Today in many religious circles, various churches, but most often in individual people's hearts they are bringing a Cain type sacrifice to the Lord. They are bringing vegetables to the Lord.

Many people think all they must do is just start going to church, give to a church, work in the church and all is well with their soul. Sadly, the truth is that none of these activities will be sufficient. Because we must be, as Jesus told Nicodemus, be "born again." Too many religious people today don't have a clue as what it is to be born again.

Any person not having experienced the new birth is bringing vegetables to the Lord...

Being born again is an experience that happens personally in an individual's life when they respond to the Holy Spirit inviting them to surrender their life to God for the performance of God's will. When the Holy Spirit draws us to God our response must be that we have faith that Jesus' sacrifice at Calvary was the sacrifice that paid for all sins ever to be committed by anyone and everyone in the world. Then we must personally accept in our hearts what Jesus accomplished with His sacrifice. This is what we refer to as saving faith. As Abel's sacrifice was made in faith we must have faith to believe and accept Christ's sacrifice. Any person not having experienced the new birth is bringing vegetables to the Lord with all their actions and religious endeavors.

The most heartbreaking thing about those bringing vegetables to the Lord is that they are unaware that they are doing so. They were baptized as an infant or very small child and knew not what it was for. Then there are many who just decided it was time to start going to church and nothing more was required to make you a Christian. The great preacher Billy Sunday said, "Going to church doesn't make you a Christian any more than going to a garage makes you an automobile."

The personal relief that comes into a person's heart when they accept Jesus, that knowing something took place in their heart that has made them a different person with different goals, different priorities, and a different outlook and focus all makes them feel anew.

They are rejuvenated, changed and simply put "made a new creature in Christ Jesus. Old things have passed away and all things are become new."

If you have never experienced that and are trying to be a Christian then you are bringing vegetables to the Lord. God doesn't want vegetables. He wants what is required. Come before Him in faith as Abel knowing what God requires giving of yourself from the experience your faith gave you.

"Come unto me all ye that are heavy laden and I will give you rest." Come believing, accepting, and confessing. This He requires.

Rev. David Trusty
Pastor of the McGuffey FWB Church

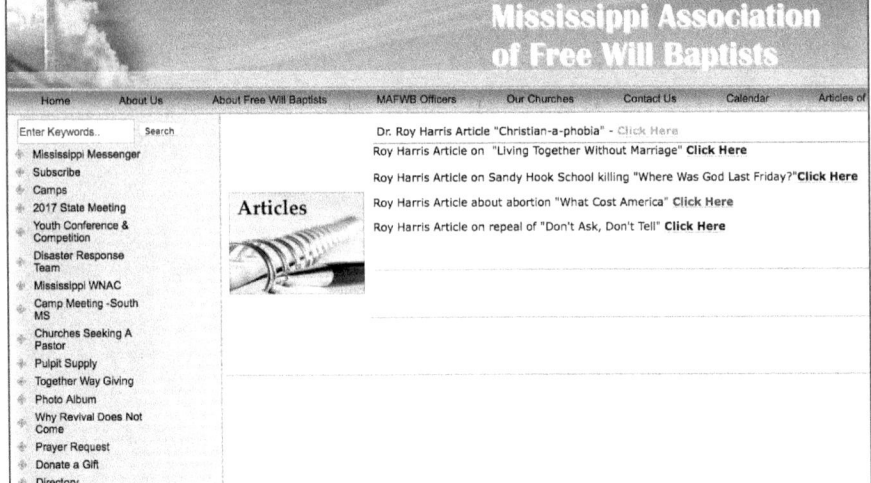

Mississippi Association of Free Will Baptists

| Home | About Us | About Free Will Baptists | MAFWB Officers | Our Churches | Contact Us | Calendar | Articles of |

Enter Keywords.. | Search

- Mississippi Messenger
- Subscribe
- Camps
- 2017 State Meeting
- Youth Conference & Competition
- Disaster Response Team
- Mississippi WNAC
- Camp Meeting -South MS
- Churches Seeking A Pastor
- Pulpit Supply
- Together Way Giving
- Photo Album
- Why Revival Does Not Come
- Prayer Request
- Donate a Gift
- Directory
- Links

VERSE OF THE DAY:
O give thanks unto the LORD, for he is good: for his mercy endureth for ever.
-- Psalm 107:1

Articles

Dr. Roy Harris Article "Christian-a-phobia" - Click Here
Roy Harris Article on "Living Together Without Marriage" **Click Here**
Roy Harris Article on Sandy Hook School killing "Where Was God Last Friday?" **Click Here**
Roy Harris Article about abortion "What Cost America" **Click Here**
Roy Harris Article on repeal of "Don't Ask, Don't Tell" **Click Here**

WHAT IS YOUR BOSS REALLY THINKING?

Get a fresh start in workplace
RELATIONS FOR 2015

By Dr. Roy W. Harris

"Please come by my office," says your boss. "I need to talk with you a minute."

Immediately your mind begins to take inventory of possible reasons for the meeting that will soon take place. You've met with the boss on numerous occasions for a variety of reasons. What could it be this time?

Have you ever wondered what the boss might be thinking during that speech she gives you, or when he gives an assignment and then frowns and waits for you to talk? What about when she goes on a rant, or when he changes company policy?

Well, from the point of view of someone who has been a boss for many years, I'll share some simple clues below that may help you better understand your boss and also help your boss to better understand you.

- Remember that the boss is always the boss. Respect the position even if you have less respect for the person than the position.

- The way you approach the boss may directly impact the way he approaches you. If your tone or body language is sarcastic or defensive, the boss may immediately place himself on the defensive. A small matter may become bigger than it should. Stop, breath, think before you speak.

- Don't take everything the boss says personally. A laugh or comment by the boss may only be an indication of a need for more information on the boss's part. Most of us make one major mistake: we think everything that the boss says or does is about us.

- Let the boss guide the conversation. You may get a clearer picture of what the boss is thinking by listening to what he or she says. Pay close attention to the words and not what you are going to say when you get an opening. Be careful about interrupting the boss (or, for that matter, any coworker).

- Find out what the boss is thinking by asking questions. Most bosses welcome appropriate questions, which will enable them better clarify their expectations and wishes. Questions like: Were you thinking something different? What would you suggest? How might I approach this? Could you give a little more detail about what you are thinking? Etc.

- Be observant of the boss's demeanor. Does he seem agitated or nervous? This could be an indication that he may have only a few minutes to talk with you or he has a pressing appointment or deadline. Remember, there is a lot of weight of responsibility on his or her shoulders. It may be better to excuse yourself and return later.

- Remember most bosses don't like surprises, especially when they contain bad news. Bosses will not only be upset with the bad news, but they will also be upset when they don't receive a heads up beforehand.

- Be humble. Proverbs 25:6-7 provides good advice. These verses encourage us to not exalt or promote ourselves in front of others, but to approach those in authority with humility. It's always better to let praise of yourself come out of someone else's mouth.

These approaches may grate against our hard driving instincts, living as we do in a very self-promotional culture, but ask yourself: who are the people you admire and value most at work? Aren't they the hard workers who value the opinions of others, don't make everything about themselves, think creatively to solve problems, respect authority, and don't toot their own horns?

Do yourself a favor this year and try to look at your workplace attitude through the eyes of a boss.

THE VISION

THE OFFICIAL PUBLICATION OF ARKANSAS FREE WILL BAPTISTS

Hey, We're Excited!

Theme:
"Because I Can!"

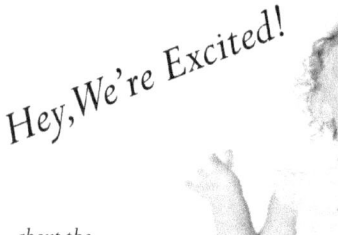

about the ...

2011 Camp Retreats

Kid's Retreat
February 25-26
Speaker: Jon Forrest

Jon is the youth pastor at Bethel Free Will Baptist Church in Ashland City, TN. He has a gift in working with children and is especially effective in presenting the gospel to those who have reached the age of accountability. He will also be leading the music during the retreat.

Teen Retreat
March 4-5
Speaker: Neil Gilliland

Neil is a sought after speaker in the FreeWill Baptist denomination and is gifted in connecting with teens. He is adjunct professor at FreeWill Baptist Bible College and has worked with Truth & Peace, Yet, and E-Team participants for many years.

Rejoice from FreeWill Baptist Bible College will be providing the music.

$25 per person for each retreat
Registration begins on Friday at 5:30 p.m.

NOTE: We are asking each person to bring 2 can or boxed goods for a food drive to be given to the Florence Crittenton Home in Little Rock. This will go to help stock their pantry. Let's give back ... BecauseWe Can!

JANUARY 2011　　　　VOLUME 53 NUMBER 1

When It's Time to Move

By Roy W. Harris

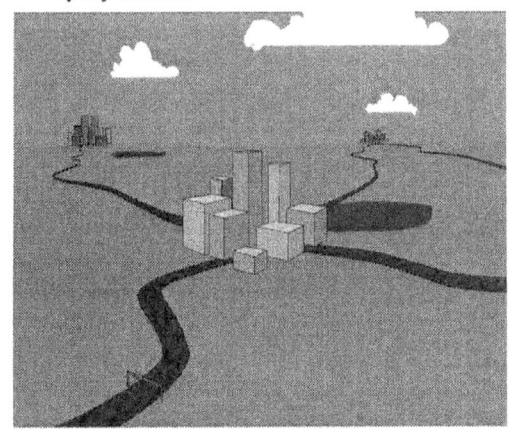

A Brief Look Back

Free Will Baptist Bible College began in 1942 with the purchase of one building for $15,000 and no assurance that the college would succeed. That fall eight students enrolled at the new denominational school. God has multiplied one building and eight students into 16 buildings and thousands of students. God has certainly been good to FWBBC and the entire Free Will Baptist denomination.

Society has changed over the last 54 years and so has FWBBC. The makeup of the student body has changed. A larger percentage of Bible College students now live in the dormitories compared to previous years.

The neighborhood where the college is located has also changed. New neighbors have moved in, and they are not as appreciative of the Bible College as those who preceded them. The college's buildings are aging. The last new building was built in the early 1970s. Many of the other buildings were built around the turn of the century.

Relocation Progress

The Land

In September 1994, the college purchased 123 acres of choice land near Joelton, Tennessee, in metropolitan Nashville/Davidson County. The property is bordered on one side by Interstate 24 and on the other side by US 41-A. The college borrowed money from itself for the initial purchase of the land, realizing that a campaign would have to be launched to repay the borrowed money.

The "Claim The Land" campaign was launched a few weeks later with the goal of repaying the money by May 31, 1996. The plan was to underwrite the land cost by encouraging Free Will Baptists to purchase the land, one acre at a time, for $3,400 per acre. The first acre was purchased in October 1994 and a commitment on the final acre came in January 1996 some four-and-a-half months ahead of the target date.

Well over a quarter of a million dollars had been received by the end of March 1996. An additional $160,000 should be received in the next few years as folks continue to pay on their commitments.

The Neighbors

The college has had a good relationship with its neighbors for many years. FWBBC has tried to "go the extra mile" to be a good neighbor and asset to the community. Many neighbors who knew the college and appreciated what the college stands for have either passed away or moved from the community.

New neighbors have moved here in the last 10 to 15 years. They seem to appreciate our students, but they have also shown that they wish to control what the college can do with its buildings and property. These neighbors have a great deal of influence. Lawyers, bankers and a city councilman live on the main street of our campus, Richland Avenue.

Some of these neighbors have formed a neighborhood association which seeks to protect and preserve the aesthetic integrity of the neighborhood. They have been successful in a rezoning effort to place the neighborhood, including our campus, under a conservation overlay. Changes to present buildings, the construction of new buildings and the demolition of any building must meet guidelines set forth in the overlay.

One of the primary reasons the overlay was sought, we feel, was to limit the further development by the college in the neighborhood and also to limit development by those who may want to purchase the college. We were told that we could not sell our present campus to another similar institution because the permit to operate the college was conditional.

After some research by our lawyer and the chairman of the Planning and Zoning Board, we learned that all our property which was purchased before 1960 was zoned for unconditional use, meaning that the heart of our campus—Davidson Hall, Memorial Auditorium, Johnson Classroom Building, Polston Hall, Ennis Hall, and the gym—sit on property purchased before the 1960 zoning changes were made.

The result is that the main institutional buildings can be sold to another like institution and used for a similar purpose. The God of Heaven is wise and knows all events that will happen in the future. He has once again shown us that He is in control and is active in the affairs of His children.

The Buyers

Several parties have shown an interest in our present campus. Potential buyers have been waiting to see if the conservation overlay would pass the City Council and, if so, what impact it would have on the value of the campus.

The college has also been waiting. We had to know what effect an overlay would have on the value of our campus. We also had to know if we could sell the campus to another like institution before we could aggressively market it. We now have some answers to our questions and are prepared to move forward.

Stage One of the relocation plan, adopted by the National Association in July 1995, has been virtually completed. Stage One called for repaying the land purchase funds, adopting a long-range plan for a phased relocation, developing a master plan for the new campus, soliciting offers for the West End property, and securing of the blessing of the National Association for the relocation of the Bible College. All of these have been done or are being done.

The Details

We are ready to proceed to Stage Two. We must continue to solicit offers for our present campus. Stage Two contains four basic elements.

1. Plan and implement a capital campaign to cover the differences, if any, between the expected selling price of the West End property and the cost of developing the new campus. This will be the next step toward relocation. More will be said about this in the months to come.

2. Authorize detailed drawings (blueprints) of all new buildings. This would be paid for with funds received through the capital campaign.

3. Develop a plan detailing the continued operation of the college while the new campus is being constructed. This will be done only after a buyer has been found. The plan will be based on the chronology of the buildings being constructed and the need to surrender buildings on our present campus to their new owner(s).

4. Finalize the details for the sale of the West End property.

Actual construction will begin in Stage Three.

Our Next Step

We are now aggressively marketing the West End campus with the hope that a buyer can be found soon. We can also move ahead with the planning and implementing of a capital campaign to help pay for detailed drawings which will be needed before actual construction can begin.

We desire the prayers of our Free Will Baptist people. Pray that God will give wisdom and direction to all who

are involved in the relocation process. The college will also need the financial support of its friends and alumni. Hundreds of thousands of dollars had to be raised to purchase the land. It will take millions to build a new campus.

Pray that God will send a buyer who can appreciate the college's need to continue to operate while a new campus is being constructed and will be willing to work with college officials to that end.

Pray that God will again touch the hearts of those who can help the college in a special way financially. It will take gifts of every size to make a new campus a reality. Pray that God will impress some individuals to underwrite the cost of an entire building. There are some among us who could do it. Pray that they will be sensitive to God's direction and leading.

We must be practical in our approach, purposeful in our planning and patient in our timing if we are to see God repeat the miracle He performed when Free Will Baptist Bible College began in 1942. God is not short on miracles. He still has at least one more for FWBBC. ■

ABOUT THE WRITER: Reverend Roy Harris directs the department of stewardship at Free Will Baptist Bible College.

July 1996, Contact **5**

The Menorah

July, 2010

Coming Events

National Association of Free Will Baptists
Oklahoma City, OK
July 18-21, 2010

Fellowship District Association
August 7, 9:00 a.m.
Community Free Will Baptist Church
6945 McKean Road
Ypsilanti, MI 48197
Rev. Don Viers, Pastor
Rev. Mike Trimble, Moderator

Liberty District Association
August 7, 9:30 a.m.
North Warren Free Will Baptist Church
3003 Chicago Road
Warren, MI 48092
Rev. George Johnson, Pastor/Moderator

West Michigan District Association
August 7, 9:30 a.m.
First Free Will Baptist Church
630 Moline
Comstock, MI 49001
Rev. John Vick, Pastor
Rev. James Williams, Associate Pastor
Rev. Bill Hughes, Moderator

Miracle in Chicago
by
Roy W. Harris
www.royharris.info

The morning began like many for the preacher. I had shaved, showered, packed and was ready to catch a plane home to Nashville. I had just finished an enjoyable four days of ministering in Michigan. Ron, Gene and Joe had welcomed me into their church pulpits. God had blessed in each service. It was great to see and preach to many men I'd come to know and appreciate at the Michigan State Minister's and Laymen's Retreat. I preached seven times in four days and enjoyed each opportunity. Joe picked me up at the hotel and we stopped a local diner for a great breakfast on the way to the airport.

I boarded the plane and it pushed away from the gate. The pilot announced that our plane would need deicing before takeoff. I had a short connection time in Chicago and was periodically looking at my watch as we waited our turn. Finally after forty minutes, we raced down the runway and were airborne. The flight was uneventful but I had a nagging concern that I might miss the connection in Chicago. I exited the plane and quickly realized my next flight was on the opposite end of the airport. I almost ran to the other side of the airport. Ah.... Relief, the Nashville flight had not boarded yet. I had made my connection. I parked my computer bag, pulled off my winter coat, reached for my cell phone....... then woke up in the Emergency Room of Holy Cross Hospital.

I didn't know where I was or what had happened. When I opened my eyes, seated next to me was a nice blond lady whom I did not recognize. She introduced herself as Rachael Jacobs and said she was a flight attendant from Southwest Airlines. I believe I asked her where I was and what was happening. She began to recount a story that was nothing short of a miracle.

Rachael was off duty and on her way to Nashville to visit her parents. She was making small talk with the desk personnel in the gate area waiting for the flight to board. A passenger came to the desk reporting a man sick and needing assistance. Rachael found me slumped over, eyes rolled back in my head and blood leaking from one corner of my mouth. Her Southwest training kicked in. She took charge, yelled back to the desk to call the paramedics and summoned the surrounding men to help her pull my wedged arm from between the seats. They move my unconscious body to the floor. Thinking this was a diabetic seizure, the normal protocol was to lay the person on the floor and let his or her body recover on its' own. Rachael did something that went directly against her training. She called for a heart defibrillator. As she recounted this part of the

1

Miracle in Chicago
By Roy W. Harris

The morning began like many for the preacher. I had shaved, showered, packed and was ready to catch a plane home to Nashville. I had just finished an enjoyable four days of ministering in Michigan. Ron, Gene and Joe had welcomed me into their church pulpits. God had blessed in each service. It was great to see and preach to many men I'd come to know and appreciate at the Michigan State Minister's and Laymen's Retreat. I preached seven times in four days and enjoyed each opportunity. Joe picked me up at the hotel and we stopped a local diner for a great breakfast on the way to the airport.

I boarded the plane and it pushed away from the gate. The pilot announced that our plane would need de-icing before takeoff. I had a short connection time in Chicago and was periodically looking at my watch as we waited our turn. Finally after forty minutes, we raced down the runway and were airborne. The flight was uneventful but I had a nagging concern that I might miss the connection in Chicago. I exited the plane and quickly realized my next flight was on the opposite end of the airport. I almost ran to the other side of the airport. Ah.... Relief, the Nashville flight had not boarded yet. I had made my connection. I parked my computer bag, pulled off my winter coat, reached for my cell phone……. then woke up in the Emergency Room of Holy Cross Hospital.

I didn't know where I was or what had happened. When I opened my eyes, seated next to me was a nice blond lady whom I did not recognize. She introduced herself as Rachael Jacobs and said she was a flight attendant from Southwest Airlines. I believe I asked her where I was and what was happening. She began to recount a story that was nothing short of a miracle.

Rachael was off duty and on her way to Nashville to visit her parents. She was making small talk with the desk personnel in the gate area waiting for the flight to board. A passenger came to the desk reporting a man sick and needing assistance. Rachael found me slumped over, eyes rolled back in my head and blood leaking from one corner of my mouth. Her Southwest training kicked in. She took charge, yelled back to the desk to call the paramedics and summoned the surrounding men to help her pull my wedged arm from between the seats. They move my unconscious body to the floor. Thinking this was a diabetic seizure, the normal protocol was to lay the person on the floor and let his or her body recover on its' own. Rachael did something that went directly against her training. She called for a heart defibrillator. As she recounted this part of the story, a pause and sense of awe filled in her voice, "it was as though a voice told me – he needs the defibrillator, he's having a heart attack."

There happened to be a doctor and ER nurse

also waiting in the gate area on their way back to Nashville. It took about fifteen minutes for the paramedics to arrive and the shock to my heart to be applied. For fifteen minutes my brain was deprived of oxygen and my heart had stopped. For all practical purposes I had died. CLEAR ….. The electric shock jolted my body….. no pulse. CLEAR a second time….. The electric shock jolted my body again leaving small red burn circles on my chest, but they had a pulse. I literally had come back from the dead. On the gurney, into the ambulance and on the way to the hospital still unconscious and medical personnel not knowing if I would live or die.

Rachael thought I was dead. She didn't understand it, but felt impressed to go to the hospital and stay until my family could get there. She sat with me for several hours until my wife and children arrived. Southwest Airlines provided free open-ended round trip tickets for my wife, daughter and son. They reserved seats for flights to Chicago, paid their cab fare to the hospital and paid for their first night's lodging in a hotel near the hospital.

I perked up and the ER personnel at first could not believe I'd suffered a heart attack. The blood work confirmed that indeed I'd suffered a massive heart attack. A heart catheterization was scheduled for the next morning and the cardiologist shared his findings "Reverend Harris, you should not be here, you should be in the morgue" or similar words to that affect. You don't smoke, drink, no blood pressure issues, not obese, no cholesterol problems, overall – you are in good physical condition. You have what is called the widow maker. You're like an athlete who runs every day and is found on the side of the road dead of a heart attack. No apparent symptoms yet major heart issues are present. The main artery feeding the left side of your heart is 99% blocked. You also have another artery 90% blocked, two 70% blocked and another 30%, 5 blockages in all. We've inserted an artificial pump into your heart to relieve the stress on your heart. You'll have lay perfectly still through the weekend to gain some strength and we'll perform bypass surgery on Monday."

The surgery was performed and was successful taking only 3 of the normal 6-8 hours. The report was great and by evening the respirator tube had been removed and I was sitting up and eating Jell-O. By Saturday I boarded a plane back to Nashville.

I met four days later with my new Nashville cardiologist. After looking at my heart from every angle, the doctor could hardly believe what he'd found. Absolutely no damage my heart! No heart rehabilitation therapy was needed! Nine days after surgery and I was far along on my road to recovery. He even allowed me to travel three weeks later alone to California and speak at the California Free Will Baptist State Men's Retreat. God blessed and we saw 6 men saved and several other decisions for Christ.

I know you've just heard quite an unusual story. God truly performed a miracle. What makes this a miracle? First of all I normally have direct flights to and from Detroit but this trip called for a divine connection in Chicago. Secondly, Rachael Jacobs, a Cardiologist and ER nurse all were divinely selected and placed on my connecting flight in Chicago. Thirdly, God timed my heart attack perfectly on the ground rather than on the plane I'd just gotten off of or the plane I was about to get on. Fourthly, a Jewish maiden obeyed the Spirit of God and deviated from standard procedure to deliver a shock that saved my life. Fifthly, I suffered no permanent heart or brain damage despite being deprived of oxygen or blood flow for over fifteen to thirty minutes. Sixthly, my recovery fast tracked to flying across country and preaching three sermons in two churches and four sermons at a state men's retreat in less than five weeks from the day of the heart attack. Finally, God has used this episode to touch countless lives through a Southwest Airlines national radio interview (**http://www.blogsouthwest.com/podcast?page=9** Title: When Rachael Met Roy), a USA cover story (**http://www.usatoday.com/money/industries/travel/2009-10-05-flight-attendants-medical-aid_N.htm**) and countless opportunities to share with individuals and churches across America.

    I didn't see a bright light or travel down a dark tunnel. One thing I do know for sure. I experienced the protecting, guiding hand of the Lord. I never feared death and felt His divine peace that passes all understanding. I've experienced great joys and great disappointments in life. God has been with me every step of the way. Take it from one who truly has passed from death unto life, not only spiritually but in my case physically as well. Every good and perfect gift comes from the Lord. Life is a precious gift. Cherish each day and live it like it might be your last. One of those days will be. If you have doubts, just remember God's Miracle in Chicago.

Featured Speakers

Join the conversation:

Where Was God Last Friday?
By Roy W. Harris
(roy@royharris.info)

The horrific events which occurred at Sandy Hook Elementary School in Newtown, Connecticut were heart wrenching, almost like a bad dream. Events that we all wish we could wake up from and find that it did not happen. Well, we all know it's much worse than a bad dream. It's a nightmare almost beyond belief that parents and grandparents of the innocent along with a disbelieving nation are living through.

On more than one occasion when evil has visited our land we've heard the question, where was God when this happened? Insinuating that somehow God was AWOL and derelict in man's perceived role of what God's responsibilities are and what He should or should not have done. I want to attempt to address that question: *Where was God last Friday* when evil seemed to triumph and innocent young children, some fine educators and the mom of an assassin all had their lives violently stolen from them and a troubled young man took his own life?

After hearing former governor Mike Huckabee's comments on this tragedy (I give him credit for some what is mentioned below), I felt impressed to pen this article. In the 1960s an effort was begun to remove Christianity and any mention of God or Christ from the public arena including: the nation's schools, government facilities, memorials and even our public squares. Much has been said over the years about the necessity building a wall between church and state. Well, much of that wall has been completed, one brick at a time. What are some of those bricks? Our courts ushered God to the exits of our schools requiring any Word from Him, mention of Him or prayer to Him, follow Him out the doors. Our courts lend credibility to lawsuits removing manager scenes or forbidding Christmas Carols from being sung in public places. Some would have any activity considered religious be locked up tight within the walls of the church. Lawsuits are filed over Christian symbols placed at public memorials which have stood quietly and reverently for generations providing comfort to families and a reminder of the faith that carried this great nation through times of war and tragedy. We have required the Ten Commandments, the bedrock of our laws and judicial system, be removed from public display in all our government facilities. Religious organizations are required to violate their biblical beliefs and distribute *morning after* abortion pills. *Happy Holidays* is now the preferred greeting by many because mentioning Christmas contains the word Christ and that might be offensive to some. We are quickly moving away from the reason for the season and *Christ's birth* is becoming a footnote. Fearing to be viewed as intolerant, we have sanitized sin calling it by politically correct names so immoral behavior and lifestyles clearly condemned by God's Word have become acceptable and even considered normal in our culture. We have methodically been eroding the moral bedrock upon which this great nation was built.

So here we are sixty years later. Our nation has successfully shown God the door. So when our culture exhibits the behavior of a nation which has abandoned its moral foundations we may be shocked, but we should not be surprised. We should also not be surprised when national tragedies occur and a morally bankrupt culture with no core beliefs seeks to locate the God they have shunned.

So where was the God, who brought this nation into existence, delivered it through several wars, provided prosperity to its citizens and blessed and protected it beyond measure like no other nation in history? He was just beyond the public arena where we left Him. He did show up during and after the terrible tragedy at Sandy Hook Elementary School. He showed up as comforter to those who'd lost children and grandchildren. He showed up in the lives of those brave ladies who looked death in the face and died protecting the students they loved. He was with the police who went into harm's way not knowing what awaited them just inside those school doors. He even made a rare appearance at the White House where His name was invoked and His Words quoted. He showed up in churches across America and in the prayers of many for hurting families and a community shaken by tragedy.

The aftermath of this horrible event will bring a discussion of possible causes and offer solutions to ensure that it will never happen again. The culture will claim to be more enlightened. But it will not be long before the God we invited back into the public arena will be escorted quietly back to the outer parameters of our culture. I do not often agree with President Obama but I do on one subject. I agree that we cannot go on like this. I may agree with his statement but I'm sure we might disagree in the changes that need to be made. Some would say we need more laws on the books and that will solve our problem. One reminder is that there are great laws on the books already and one especially that covers this situation. It's found in those same Ten Commandments we have removed from the public view of our culture: *Thou Shall Not Kill*. I know it is not as simple as that and more needs to be said and done, but I do know that is where it should begin. God's clear prescription for a successful nation is simple and has not changed since Solomon's time and will still work today. God reminds us in 2 Chronicles 7:12; *If my people, which are called by my name, shall humble themselves, and pray, and seek my face, and turn from their wicked ways; then will I hear from heaven, and will forgive their sin, and will heal their land.* It begins with doing our *IFs* and ends with God doing His *THENs*.

So Where was God Last Friday? There are three lines from the chorus of one of Gary Paxon's songs says it pretty well. *(Chorus) He was there all the time.*
Waiting patiently in line.
He was there all the time.
Something *must* change in this nation. God is longsuffering and patient. He is still waiting. It's our move.

The greatest thing we can do for our nation is to pray for humble recognition of our need for God's divine help, for conviction of our national sins and for genuine repentance and turning from those sins. If this happens, God will help us with the rest and we can be assured that He will be with us every Friday.

FIRST DAYTON (LITTLE MIAMI)

Greetings to our brothers and sisters in Christ from First Dayton FWB Church. Now that the hustle and bustle of the holiday season is over, I hope everyone had a wonderful Christmas season with family and friends, but most of all I hope we all remembered and thanked our Heavenly Father for giving us his own Son to die on the cross for us. The true meaning - such a priceless gift.

We had our Veteran's Day service along with our Thanksgiving meal together this past November. We had a wonderful time sharing pictures, stories and videos of the veterans from our church and from the families in our church. We had a few of them with us that day as we recognized them in front of the congregation. We had a wonderful meal served to us by our young people.

First Dayton Veterans

The church had a real good turn out for the Christmas cantata. We practiced and had our Christmas service on December 23rd. We had several visitors and a wonderful service. Please remember our sick and shut-ins. Please pray for our church that we will continue to strive to do God's will and our attendance will grow and we will lead lost souls to Christ.

Robert Legg, Pastor
Jennifer Robbins, Reporter

Evangelist
Mike Blanton

Available for services, revivals and campmeetings!

(614) 871-2795

Mike Blanton and Evidence available to sing at your church!

Where Was God Last Friday
By Roy W. Harris

The horrific events, which occurred at Sandy Hook Elementary School in Newtown, Connecticut, were heart wrenching, almost like a bad dream that we all wish we could wake up from and find that it did not happen. Well, we all know it's much worse than a bad dream. It's a nightmare almost beyond belief that parents and grandparents of the innocent along with a disbelieving nation are living through.

On more than one occasion when evil has visited our land we've heard the question; where was God when this happened? Insinuating that somehow God was AWOL and derelict in man's perceived role of what God's responsibilities are and what He should or should not have done. I want to attempt to address that question: *Where was God last Friday* when evil seemed to triumph and innocent young children, some fine educators and the mom of an assassin all had their lives violently stolen from them and a troubled young man took his own life?

After hearing former governor Mike Huckabee's comments on this tragedy (I give him credit for some what is mentioned below), I felt impressed to pen this article. In the 1960s an effort was begun to remove Christianity and any mention of God or Christ from the public area including; the nation's schools, government facilities, memorials and even our public squares. Much has been said over the years about the necessity building a wall between church and state.

Well, much of that wall has been completed, one brick at a time. What are some of those bricks? Our courts ushered God to the exits of our schools requiring any Word from Him, mention of Him or prayer to Him, follow Him out the doors. Our courts lend credibility to lawsuits removing manager scenes or forbidding Christmas Carols from being sung in public places. Some would have any activity considered *religious* be locked up tight within the walls of the church. Lawsuits are filed over Christian symbols paced at public memorials that have stood quietly and reverently for generations providing comfort to families and a reminder of the faith that carried this great nation through times of war and tragedy.

We have required the Ten Commandments, the bedrock of our laws and judicial system, be removed from public display in all our government facilities. Religious organizations are required to violate their biblical beliefs and distribute *morning after* abortion pills. *Happy Holidays* is now the preferred greeting by many because mentioning Christmas contains the word Christ and that might be offensive to some. We are quickly moving away from the reason for the season and *Christ's birth* is becoming a footnote. Fearing to be viewed as intolerant, we have sanitized sin calling it by politically correct names so immoral behavior and lifestyles clearly condemned by God's Word have become acceptable and even considered normal in our culture. We have methodically been eroding the moral bedrock upon which this great nation was built.

So here we are sixty years later. Our nation has successfully shown God the door. So when our culture exhibits the behavior of a nation, which has abandoned its moral foundations we may be shocked, but we should not be surprised. We should also not be surprised when national tragedies occur and a morally bankrupt culture with no core beliefs seeks to locate the God they have shunned.

So where was the God, who brought this nation into existence, delivered it through several wars, provided prosperity to its citizens and blessed and protected it beyond measure like no other nation in history? He was just beyond the public arena where we left Him. He did show up during and after the terrible tragedy at Sandy Hook Elementary School. He showed up as comforter to those who'd lost children and grandchildren. He showed up in the lives of those brave ladies who looked death in the face and died protecting the students they loved. He was with the police who went into to harm's way not knowing what awaited them just inside those school doors. He even made a rare appearance at the White House where His name was invoked and His Words quoted. He showed up in churches across America and in the prayers of many for hurting families and a community shaken by tragedy.

The aftermath of this horrible event will bring a discussion of possible causes and offer solutions to ensure that it will never happen again. The culture will claim to be more enlightened. But it will not be long before the God we invited back into the public arena will be escorted quietly back to the outer parameters of our culture. I do not often agree with President Obama but I do on one subject. I agree that we cannot go on like this. I may agree with his statement but I'm sure we might disagree in the changes that need to be made.

Some would say we need more laws on the books and that will solve our problem. One reminder is that there are great laws on the books already and one especially that covers this situation. It's found in those same Ten Commandments we have removed from the public view of our culture: *Thou Shall Not Kill.* I know it is not as simple as that and more needs to be said and done, but I do know that is where it should begin. God's clear prescription for a successful nation is simple and has not changed since Solomon's time and will still work today.

God reminds us in 2 Chronicles 7:12; *If my people, which are called by my name, shall humble themselves, and pray, and seek my face, and turn from their wicked ways; then will I hear from heaven, and will forgive their sin, and will heal their land*. It begins with doing our *IFs* and ends with God doing His *THENs*.

So *Where was God Last Friday*? There are three lines from the chorus of one of Gary Paxon's songs says it pretty well.

(Chorus) *He was there all the time.*
Waiting patiently in line.

He was there all the time.

Something *must change* in this nation. God is longsuffering and patient. He is still waiting. It's our move.

The greatest thing we can do for our nation is to pray for humble recognition of our need for God's divine help, for conviction of our national sins and for genuine repentance and turning from those sins. If this happens, God will help us with the rest and we can be assured that He will be with us every Friday.

Reflections

FOR THE LOVE OF THE GAME

By ROY W. HARRIS

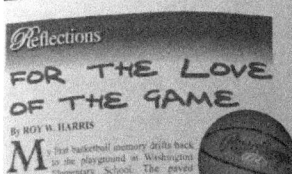

My first basketball memory drifts back to the playground at Washington Elementary School. The paved playground, metal backboard and faded nets just ran deep in me like a moth to a flame. The challenge of shooting the ball through that hoop was about to die from the heat. I didn't know much about the game, but I did know that I enjoyed it and wanted to learn more.

My second memory moved off the playground onto the hard wood floor. While shooting baskets during lunch time one day I was encouraged by Mr. Leonard, the elementary school basketball coach, to try out for the basketball team. To my surprise, I made the team. I remember receiving my uniform and wearing the yellow and blue warm up shirt to class all afternoon even though I was about to die from the heat. I didn't take it off till I arrived home after school.

Basketball was my first love. Fortunately I had a coach who loved the game for the game itself. There was purity for the game that he instilled deep within me during those early days. Thanks again Mr. Leonard. I went on to play middle school, high school and college basketball, and those basic principles formed a prism through which I came to view all sports.

With March Madness having ended, a new NCAA national champion crowned, the NBA playoffs just over the horizon, basketball is fresh on many sports fans' minds. Sports, in a way, are a snapshot of who we are. I know the good old days were never quite as good as our littered minds remember, but I believe good old day principles never go out of style. Here are a few basketball principles that you play well in the game of life.

GOOD SPORTSMANSHIP I remember hearing my coach say the most important thing is not if you win or lose but how you play the game. We worked hard in practice and were taught to play hard and give it our all every minute of the game. We were also taught to appreciate the good play of our teammates and the opposing team. Now don't get me wrong, it's a whole lot more fun winning than losing, and I'd much rather be at the top of the conference than at the cellar, but the emphasis on winning has become more important than appreciating the joy of the game. I'm troubled by those who try to take a shortcut to success by introducing performance enhancing drugs into the final score or those who try to get an advantage by unethically or illegally obtaining the other team's plays. We were taught that we should be gracious winners and good losers.

DEPORTMENT Deportment is an old word that deserves a new look. How you behaved on the court, how you looked and what you did off the court mattered. It's a bit troubling to see the lack of good deportment on the court. You never chided or made fun of your opponent's mistakes (although you did your best to take advantage of them). Often you saw players going on between plays which sometimes escalates into open brawling. Once again, a time there was a warning then a technical foul if things like that persisted. If you played hard you or your opponent would eventually end up on the floor. You always helped an opponent to his feet, and you were concerned that he might be injured. In most college and pro sports today one only helps his teammate up from a fall and never an opponent. The game seems now to dominate your opponent in every way. This is illustrated by what I call the Emancipation & Intimidation factor. The look of the player matters. Many players now sport bodacious tattoos covering most of both arms. The college players must get the pro players. In my ever so humble opinion, I believe this is a statement by the basketball player that it matters little what others think, he has freedom to do what he pleases. I think the goal is to try to intimidate the opposing players. This is America, and people are free to look and be whatever they want to be. However, I do think that since the emancipation & intimidation factor has entered the game, that the game has taken a step backwards.

TEAMWORK Bill Russell, Bob Cousy, Dr. J, Larry Bird, Magic Johnson and Michael Jordan are only a few on a list too long to name who generate visions of champions and success. Although each man was very unique each made his team better. Our coaches taught us that you are never bigger than the team. There are some sports which focus on individual achievement, golf for instance. But isn't it amazing when the Ryder Cup matches with the Europeans roll around every other year, how individual performance is measured by team success. Those individuals like Phil Mickelson and Tiger Woods become part of something bigger than themselves. I learned to pass the ball to the open man who had the best chance to make the shot. I learned to wait for my teammates on a fast break when we didn't have the numbers and to pull the ball out and until the odds evened up. Emphasis now is on the franchise player. Who is the guy who will win us a championship? No man wins a championship. Teams win championships. A guy or gal should be careful about thinking the sun rises and sets on his/her ability as a player. A truly good player makes those around him better.

Let's apply some of the above principles to everyday life.

SPORTSMANSHIP True success in life comes with how you play the game. Success comes from hard work and giving it your all. When you try to find shortcuts to success you'll end up at the back of the line of your own personal self-respect. Learn to praise those who do well and be kind and generous when you come in first.

DEPORTMENT How you carry yourself and how you behave does matter. Be known as one who cares and extends a helping hand instead of leaving it to others. You have the God given American freedom to look and do as you please, but always remember, others are watching. Lead by example. You can be emancipated without covering in tattoos. If you intimidate you are driving others to follow rather than trying to force them in another direction.

TEAMWORK Always remember you are the sum total of all those who've invested in your life. They are part of your team, of life that made you what you are today. If you want to succeed in the future, make those around you better. You might be surprised at how much you'll grow and become better yourself. Learn to love life and love others. Play by the rules. For The Love of the Game reminds us that success is measured by how well we play the game.

One day when we stand before our heavenly Father, His question will be: "How well did you play the game?" We all want to hear Him say, "Well done good and faithful servant." ◆

Spend Your Pool Time In The Water!

Backyard Living LLC
"Come outside and enjoy"

- Pool Opening - $275 (plus chemicals)
- Weekly Service - $160/mo. (plus chemicals)
New customers only, chemicals not included.

FREE 1 Month Pool Service
With Purchase of Weekly Service Contract

Other Services Offered:
Pool Service Calls • Vinyl Liner Replacement
Hot Tubs Cleaning & Service • Pool Deck Resurfacing
1 Time Cleaning for Special Events

www.BackyardLivingLLC.com   Call NOW (615) 444-90(
Pool Financing Avail

For the Love of the Game
By
Roy W. Harris

My first basketball memory drifts back to the playground at Washington Elementary School. The paved playground, metal backboard and faded netless rim drew me like a moth to a flame. The challenge of shooting the ball through that hoop was one that grew quickly. I didn't know much about the game but I did know that I enjoyed it and wanted to learn more.

My second memory moved off the playground onto the hardwood floor. While shooting baskets during lunch time one day I was encouraged by Mr. Leonard, the elementary school basketball coach to try out for the basketball team. To my surprise, I made the team. I remember receiving my uniform and wearing the yellow and blue warm up shirt to class all afternoon even though I was about to die from the heat. I didn't take it off till I arrived home after school.

Basketball was my first love. Fortunately I had a coach who loved the game for the game itself. There was purity for the game that he instilled deep within me during those early days. Thanks again Mr. Leonard. I went on to play middle school, high school and college basketball and those basic principles formed a prism through which I came to view all sports.

With *March Madness* having ending, a new NCAA

national champion crowned, the NBA playoffs just over the horizon, basketball is fresh on many sports fans minds. Sports in a way are a *snapshot* of who we are. I know the *good old days* were never quite as good as our filtered minds remember, but I believe *good old day* principles never go out of style. Here are a few basketball principles that also play well in the game of life.

Good Sportsmanship – I remember hearing my coaches say *the most important thing is not if you win or lose, but how you play the game.* We worked hard in practice and were taught to play hard and give it our all every minute of the game. We were also taught to appreciate the good play of our teammates and the opposing team. Now don't get me wrong, it's a whole lot more fun winning than losing and I'd much rather be at the top of the conference than in the cellar, but the emphasis on winning has become more important than appreciating the joy of the game. I'm troubled by those who try to take a *shortcut to success* by introducing performance enhancing drugs into the final score or those who try to get an advantage by unethically or illegally obtaining the other team's plans. We were taught that we should be gracious winners and good losers.

Deportment – Deportment is an old word that deserves a new look. How you behaved on the court, how you looked and what you did off the court mattered. It's a bit troubling to see the lack of good deportment on the court. You never chided or made light of your opponent's mistakes (although you did your best to take advantage of them). Often you see

5*jawing* going on between players that sometimes escalates into open *brawling*. Once upon a time there was a warning then a technical foul if things like that persisted. If you played hard you or your opponent would eventually end up on the floor. You always helped an opponent to his feet and you were concerned that he might be injured. In most college and pro games today, one only helps his teammate up from a fall and never an opponent. The goal seems now to dominate your opponent in every way. This is illustrated by what I call the *Emancipation & Intimidation* factor. The way players look matters.

    Many players now sport bookend tattoos covering most of both arms. The college players imitate the pro players. In my ever so humble opinion, I believe this is a statement by the individual player that it matters little what others think, he has freedom to do what he pleases. I think the goal is to try to *intimidate* the opposing players. This is America and people are free to look and be whatever they want to be. However, I do think that since the *emancipation & intimidation* factor has entered the game, that the game has taken a step backwards. Contrary to what some would have us believe, dressing down is not always the best thing.

    Teamwork – Bill Russell, Bob Cousy, Dr. J., Larry Bird, Magic Johnson and Michael Jordan are only a few on a list too long to name who generate visions of champions and success. Although each man was very unique each made his team better. Our coaches taught us that you are never bigger than the team.

There are some sports, which focus on individual achievement, golf for instance. But isn't it amazing when the Rider Cup matches with the Europeans roles around every other year how individual performance is measured by team success. Those individuals like Phil Michelson and Tiger Woods become part of something bigger than themselves. I learned to pass the ball to the open man who had the best chance to make the shot. I learned to wait for my teammates on a fast break when we didn't have the numbers and to pull the ball out and until the odds evened up. Emphasis now is on the *franchise* player. Who is the guy who will win us a championship? No man wins a championship. Teams win championships. A guy or gal should be careful about thinking the sun rises and sets on his/her ability as a player. A truly good player makes those around him better.

Let's apply some of the above principles to everyday life.

Sportsmanship – True success in life comes with *how you play the game*. Success comes from hard work and giving it your all. When you try to find *shortcuts* to success you'll end up at the back of the line of your own personal self-respect. Learn to praise those who do well and be kind and generous when you come in first. *Deportment* – How you carry yourself and how you behave does matter. Be known as one who cares and extends a helping hand instead of leaving it to others. You have the God given American freedom to look and do as you please, but always remember; *others are watching*. Lead by example. You can be *emancipated* without reverting to *intimidation.* If you *intimidate* you are driving instead of leading. It's much easier when people follow rather than trying to force them in another direction.

Teamwork – Always remember you are the sum total of all those who've invested in your life. They are part of your team of life that made you what you are today. If you want to succeed in the future, make those around you better. You might be surprised how much you'll grow and become better yourself. Learn to love life and love others. Play by the rules. For The Love of the Game reminds us that success is measured by how well we play the game. One day when we stand before our heavenly Father, His question will be; how well did you play the game? We want to hear Him say, *well done that good and faithful servant.*

ONE MAGAZINE

The Magazine for Free Will Baptists

CONTACT INFORMATION SUBSCRIBE LINKS

June-July 2015

Interface: Make the Connection

Online Edition
Download PDF
iPad and eReader

History Resources
About

Why Tithe?

By Roy W. Harris

I tithe because my parents did.

Why Tithe

By Roy W. Harris

I Tithe Because My Parents Did.

The Sunday morning began like most. We finished breakfast. Mom was putting the final touches on her lady-like appearance. Dad, my brother Rick and I were in the den watching The Gospel Jubilee providing us with a enjoyable mix of Southern Gospel Music from The Blackwood Brothers, The Goodman Family and numerous other singers.

Dad, leaning forward in his recliner, picked up his checkbook from an end table. He filled out a check paid to the order of: First Free Will Baptist Church, Anderson, Indiana. He signed, folded and placed the check in his shirt pocket. He would later slip it from his pocket and drop in an offering plate as an act of worship during the Sunday morning Worship Service.

I was in my mid-teens but I remember this Sunday morning routine well. This was not the first time I witnessed this act. This was Dad's *practice* every Sunday morning for as long as I can remember.

Why do I tithe? My parents taught me to tithe. They believed in and practiced tithing when I was a boy, and 45 years later they still do. They talked about tithing in front my brother and me. They told us why they tithed.

They described ways in which God had blessed our family because they tithed. They even scared us a little by mentioning others who they knew didn't tithe and how those people paid the tithe in medical bills, car repairs and other unforeseen personal expenses.

They made such a strong case for tithing that my brother and I didn't know we couldn't tithe as boys growing up in Albert Harris' household.

I Tithe because I know tithing is a good investment.

I remember reading Malachi chapter three in my early days as a student at Welch College. I'd read that passage before, but now I was in college away from my tithing parents and had begun choosing my own path in life.

God spoke to my heart that day in a direct and meaningful way. I understood Him to say through His Word: *"Roy, why not test me. If you'll be faithful in tithing, I'll take care of all your needs and give you more than you can imagine for the rest of your life. I'll take what you give me, multiply it and then give back much more to you than you've given me."* (Malachi 3:10-12)

I made a commitment to God that day and believed in His commitment to me. I've remained faithful to my tithing commitment for over forty years and I can say without hesitations that God not only kept His commitment to me, but He has given me far more than I could have imagined when I was that eighteen-year-old young man.

I've made numerous investments in a variety of venues, which have produced good results. I can truly say the greatest investment that has yielded the best return is the heavenly investment of the tithe and offering.

I Tithe because the Bible tells me to.

God's holy Word is clear on the matter of tithing. There are numerous sources that give detailed descriptions and scriptural evidence for God's requirement of the tithe from every Christian believer.

I think Malachi 3:8-9 is sufficient here to reinforce God's demand for the tithe. God instructs us in verse eight that men rob God when they do not give tithes and offerings.

It's a dangerous thing to steal from God. How dangerous? I wouldn't want to offend the one who holds my entire financial future in His hands. Verse nine says those who rob God pay a heavy price. Instead of receiving God's favor and blessings, they are cursed and will receive God's disfavor.

I Tithe because it is God's plan for supporting the local church.

God instructs us in Malachi 3:10 to bring the tithes into the storehouse. Obviously, the local church is God's modern day storehouse and is the depository for the currency of the tithe. I give my tithe to my local church and then give my offerings to wherever God directs.

I do not have to pray about the minimum I should give or where I should give it! God has clearly defined that in his Word. A minimum of 10% of my income is to be given to my local church. From there, the sky is the limit on how much and where to give offerings.

Should you Tithe?

Parents please remember, your children are watching. They will *do as you do* rather than *do as you say.* Parents want children to enjoy the best life they possibly can afford. The most beneficial financial package and legacy parents can leave their children are examples of Jesus Christ in every way and that includes *returning the tithe* and *giving an offering* above the tithe.

You may wonder why I used the word *return* the tithe instead of *give*? The simple truth is the tithe *already belongs* to God. We actually *begin giving,* when the tithe has been returned to God. The *offering* follows the *tithe* and becomes an offering once the tithe threshold has been met and is returned to God.

Want a hot tip on a good investment? Learn to live on 90% of the 100% God gives you. Put God to the test. Return the 10% that *belongs* to Him and watch how He will multiply it and give back to you above and beyond what you thought or imagined.

The scriptures teach us that *God loves a cheerful giver.* Want to make God happy? Return the tithe to Him, as recognition that you understand the 100% you receive is His gift to you.

Give and offering above the tithe as God directs you to show your appreciation for all He sends your way. You might be surprised what a wonderful satisfying feeling you experience each time you *return the tithe* and *give and offering*.

Why do I Tithe? A better question might be: *Why wouldn't I?* What about you?

Cicada Time in Tennessee

by ROY W. HARRIS

Every year Memorial Day weekend officially kicks off one of the most looked forward to times of the year – SUMMER. Nature moves into high gear with greening lawns, leafing trees and exploding color of flowering mosaics that only the fingers of God could create. This year's announcement of impending summer brought with it something else, the arrival of an unusual insect known as the Cicada. Cicadas are not new to those of us who've been around middle Tennessee for more than a dozen years but to others they are strange creatures that look like a cross between a dragonfly and a grasshopper who lost his back legs.

Only the good Lord knows the reason and purpose of the Cicadas. Their lives seem to be characterized by little purpose, enjoyment or fulfillment. They come from nowhere, stick around for a few weeks, eat, breed, crawl back into the ground and are not heard from for another thirteen years.

Why mention Cicadas? Maybe there are lessons we can learn from the Cicada. Let's give it a shot – "Lessons from the Cicadas".

Lesson #1. Life is short. The Cicada is on this earth for a short period of time. The scriptures tell us that most people are lucky if they live to be 70 and doubly so if they reach 80. The years quickly pass and like the Cicada, we fly away. According to 2011 U.S. statistics, life expectancy for the average American is 78.3 years. Isn't it amazing that something written thousands of years ago is still accurate today. The scriptures also compare the length of life to a vapor or wisp of steam. We seem to suddenly appear on this earth, and just as quickly disappear and are gone. Our time on earth is short. We should make our lives count for worthwhile things which have eternal value.

Lesson #2. Life has purpose. For the life of me I cannot find a reason for the existence of the Cicada. Even though it may be hidden from us, God has purpose in everything He does, and He has a purpose and reason for the clockwork like 13-year arrival of the Cicada.

The scriptures remind us that every human being is uniquely created by God and his or her clock-like arrival on this earth is an appointment with destiny prearranged by God Himself. Others may never know, and we may never fully understand what our purpose is, but we can rest in the assurance that God has a pre-designed plan for each of us.

Lesson #3. Life has choices. The Cicada male makes a sound which has been clocked at over 100 decibels. The united chorus of thousands of male Cicadas radiates like loud speakers from every tree and shrub in the neighborhood. The males sound off in an attempt to attract the attention of a potential mate. The female has an almost limitless choice of males to choose from. Who knows why she picks out that perfect one? Our lives are also filled with choices. Our choices are influenced by a myriad of voices radiating from a variety of people and circumstances. Doing the right thing is always the right thing to do. How do we make right choices? The Cicada has to rely on nature's instinct. We have two wonderful gifts provided to help us. One is our conscience. God has placed a sense of right and wrong deep down inside each of us. The arrow our moral compass points us towards is magnetic right and 180 degrees away from moral wrong. Letting your conscience be your guide is pretty safe for most situations. God also offers wisdom from above. Solomon, considered to be one of the wisest men who ever lived, wrote a book found in the Bible called Proverbs. It provides a wealth of practical advice for our daily choices. A great way to gain wisdom for life is to read one chapter in Proverbs each day (Proverbs has 31 chapters). Reading one chapter per day will help one to gain insight into how to be healthy, wealthy and wise. Well, maybe wise anyway.

Lesson #4. Life has opportunities. The Cicadas live their short lives exhibiting a philosophy that seems far too prevalent in our world today. That philosophy is that it's all about me. The Cicada lives his life grabbing for himself, never giving – only taking. There is no greater feeling in the world than giving. The recent flooding of those along the Mississippi River is a reminder of the great 1,000-year flood we experienced a little over a year ago in middle Tennessee. There was little self-pity or looking towards Washington for help. There was an immediate onslaught of volunteers who mobilized wanting to help those who'd been devastated by floodwaters. The spirit of giving and expecting nothing in return became the order of the day. That biblical principle that 'it is more blessed to give than to receive' still rings true today. We each have opportunities to give time, talent and treasure to our families, friends, church, community and nation. Another expression we've heard is 'give till it hurts'. I believe a greater principle is the promise in scripture; 'give and it will be given unto you'. Giving generates a lasting feeling of satisfaction that only taking can never produce.

The Cicadas have come and gone one more time. Maybe one of God's purposes for sending them was to teach us another lesson or two about life. Whatever their purpose – it will be another thirteen years before we hear from them again. I must say – I'm not disappointed that they are gone.

Roy W. Harris is a marriage seminar and retreat speaker, minister, published author and journalist. He can be contacted by email at roy@royharris.info or visit his website at www.royharris.info.

Cicada Time in Tennessee

By Roy W. Harris

Every year Memorial Day weekend officially kicks off one of the most looked forward to times of the year – SUMMER. Nature moves into high gear with greening lawns, leafing trees and exploding color of flowering mosaics that only the fingers of God could create. This year's announcement of impending summer brought with it something else, the arrival of an unusual insect known as the Cicada. Cicadas are not new to those of us who've been around middle Tennessee for more than a dozen years but to others they are strange creatures that look like a cross between a dragonfly and a grasshopper that lost his back legs.

Only the good Lord knows the reason and purpose of the Cicadas. Their lives seem to be characterized by little purpose, enjoyment or fulfillment. They come from nowhere, stick around for a few weeks, eat, breed, crawl back into the ground and are not heard from for another thirteen years.
Why mention Cicadas? Maybe there are lessons we can learn from the Cicada. Let's give it a shot – **"Lessons from the Cicadas."**

Lesson #1. **Life is short**. The Cicada is on this earth for a short period of time. The scriptures tell us in that most people are lucky if they live to be 70 and doubly so it they reach 80. The years quickly pass and like the Cicada, we fly away. According to 2011 U.S statistics, life expectancy for the average American is

78.3 years. Amazing isn't it how something written thousands of years ago is still accurate today. The scriptures also compare the length of life to a vapor or wisp of steam. We seem to suddenly appear on this earth and just as quickly disappear and are gone. Our time on earth is short. We should make our lives count for worthwhile things, which have eternal value.

Lesson #2. **Life has purpose.** For the life of me I cannot find a reason for the existence of the Cicada. Even though it may be hidden from us, God has purpose in everything He does and He has a purpose and reason for the clockwork like 13-year arrival of the Cicada. The scriptures remind us that God uniquely creates every human being and his/her clocklike arrival on this earth is an appointment with destiny prearranged by God Himself. Others may never know and we may never fully understand what our purpose is, but we can rest in the assurance that God has a predesigned plan for each of us.

Lesson #3. **Life has choices.** The Cicada male makes a sound that has been clocked at over 100 decibels. The united chorus of thousands of male Cicadas radiates like loud speakers from every tree and shrub in the neighborhood. The males sound off in an attempt to attract the attention of a potential mate. The female has an almost limitless choice of males to choose from. Who knows why she picks out that perfect one? Our lives are also filled with choices. Our choices are influenced by a myriad of voices radiating from a variety of people and circumstances. Doing *the right thing* is always *the right thing* to do. How do we make right choices? The Cicada has to rely on nature's instinct. We have two wonderful gifts provided to help us. One is our conscience. God has placed a sense of right and wrong deep down inside each of us. The arrow our *moral compass* points us towards *magnetic right* and 180 degrees away from *moral wrong*. *Let your conscience be your guide* is pretty safe for most situations. God also offers *wisdom from above.* Solomon, considered to be one of the wisest men who ever lived, wrote a book found in the bible called Proverbs. It provides a wealth of practical advice for our daily choices. A great way to gain wisdom for life is to read one chapter in Proverbs each day (Proverbs has 31 chapters). Reading one chapter per day will help one to gain insight into how to be *healthy, wealthy* and *wise.* Well, maybe *wise* anyway.

Lesson #4. **Life has opportunities.** The Cicadas live their short lives exhibiting a philosophy that seems far too prevalent in our world today. That philosophy is that *it's all about me*. The Cicada lives his life *grabbing for* himself, never giving – only taking. There is no greater feeling in the world than *giving*. The recent flooding of the along the Mississippi River is a reminder of the great 1,000 year flood we experienced a little over a year ago in middle Tennessee. There was little self-pity or looking towards Washington for help. There was an immediate onslaught of volunteers who mobilized wanting to help those who'd been devastated by floodwaters. The spirit of *giving* and expecting nothing in return became the order of the day. That biblical principle that *It is more blessed to give than to receive* still rings true today. We each have opportunities to give *time, talent* and *treasure* to our families, friends, church, community and nation. Another expression we've heard is *Give till it hurts.* I believe a greater principle is the promise in scripture; *give and it will be given unto you. Giving* generates a lasting feeling of satisfaction that only taking can never produce.

The Cicadas have come and gone one more time. Maybe one of God's purposes for sending them was to teach us another lesson or two about life. Whatever their purpose – it will be another thirteen years before we hear from them again. I must say – I'm not disappointed that they are gone.

Reflections

Kindergarten Forgiveness

By ROY W. HARRIS

1958 Kindergarten Class

Labor Day was once the point of demarcation for all school age children signaling the end of summer fun and the beginning of another nine months of new classrooms, new teachers, new classmates and evenings of homework. School year schedules have changed and many school systems begin classes a month before Labor Day and some continue with extended schedules throughout the year.

Can you remember your first day of school? I remember mine well. I was a short, redheaded, freckle faced five-year-old little boy on my way to kindergarten. Jerry Swallows, a playmate of mine was also headed on this great new adventure with me. The Simmons boys, who lived two houses up the street from us, had prepped me for the biggest event in my short young life. In great detail they warned me of the horrors that awaited little unsuspecting boys. They alerted me to watch out for one thing in particular. Located on the outskirts of our town was a Reform School, a home for delinquent children as they were called in those days. We passed it each time we drove to the park. The Simmons boys told me that my elementary school officials would pick out certain little boys, make them line up and then follow a woman out of the room. Those boys would then be driven to Reform School and would never see their parents again.

Washington School – Where Roy spent his first day of school

We passed through the front doors of the elementary school and mom dropped me off with the other five-year-olds. We were sequestered in a big room. Well, you guessed it. They announced that if your name was called that you were to get in line and follow Miss so and so. I began to cry and did not want to go. I told Jerry to please tell my mom goodbye for me. What a mean, dirty trick for older boys to play on an innocent, trusting and unsuspecting little boy. Obviously, the school officials had so many five-year-olds that they were dividing the group into classes, and each one of us were assigned to follow our new teacher to our new classroom. You will never know how wonderful it felt to see my mom walk through the door and pick me up later in the day.

I was really scared by the whole ordeal. I didn't tell anyone about it, but I never forgot it. I've gotten over it, but I still have a little chill run down my spine when I enter elementary schools (not really). I moved on, forgave the Simmons boys, and Marcus (aka Bug) became one of my closest neighborhood friends.

All of us can relate experiences about when people have done us wrong. I can remember telling my parents, "that isn't fair." In a perfect world no one would ever deceive, mistreat or hurt anyone else. But unfortunately we do not live in a perfect world, and life certainly is not always fair.

One of the hardest things in life to do, is forgive. It seems to come more easily to children. They forgive little conflicts with their siblings and playmates. Within minutes the whole affair is forgotten, and they are playing together again. With adults, it is not as simple. The older we get, the harder it seems to be to forgive. Forgiveness is an act that does as much, if not more, for the forgiver as the forgiven.

What does forgiving someone who has wronged us, do for us? It frees us from the control of the "once hurt they've caused us." Many times people who've mistreated us don't lose three seconds sleep over the whole matter. We may carry it for days, months and yes, even years. They forget completely about it, but we relive it over and over again. We are captivated in the prison of our own thoughts. A decision to forgive, even though the person may not have asked for forgiveness, frees us from the prison of our own hurt feelings and helps us move on with life.

Forgiveness is an essential part of a warm and happy marriage. It was once said that a happy marriage is the union of two good forgivers. Forgiveness is essential in the work place if we are to get along with people and learn to be content with our jobs. Forgiveness is essential with our neighbors. I once knew of two ladies who didn't speak to each other for over twenty years because one lady's chickens strayed into the garden of the other. What a waste. Twenty years of friendship sacrificed over some chickens and tomatoes. Forgiveness is essential on the highway. I know there are bad drivers out there who cut us off and do inconsiderate things. Forgiving at that moment may keep us from saying or doing something we may regret later.

The scriptures teach us that if we want peace and God's forgiveness, then we must forgive others. It is not easy, and it sometimes takes us a while to arrive there. But we are the winners when we forgive. We have much to gain when we forgive others and much to lose when we do not. So don't stay in the prison of hurt and mistreated feelings. Forgive early, forgive generously, forgive completely and forgive eternally. You'll be the WINNER. Remember that old saying: "To err is human, to forgive is divine."

Roy is a national Conference, Seminar and Retreat speaker and can be contacted at Roy@royharris.info or view his website at www.royharris.info

Kindergarten Forgiveness

By Roy W. Harris

Labor Day was once the *point of demarcation* for all school age children signaling the end of summer fun and the beginning of another nine months of new classrooms, new teachers, new classmates and evenings of homework. School year schedules have changed and many school systems begin classes a month before Labor Day and some continue with extended schedules throughout the year.

Can you remember your first day of school? I remember mine well. I was a short red headed, freckle faced five year old little boy on my way to kindergarten. Jerry Swallows a playmate of mine was also headed on this great new adventure with me. The Simmons boys who live two houses up the street from us had prepped me for the coming biggest event in my short young life. In great detail they warned me of the horrors that awaited little unsuspecting boys. They alerted me to watch out for one thing in particular. Located on the outskirts of our town was a *Reform School,* a home for *delinquent* children as they called in those days. We passed it each time we drove to the park. The Simmons boys told me that my elementary school officials would pick out certain little boys, make them line up and then follow a woman out of the room. Those boys would then be driven to *Reform School* and never see their parents again.

We passed through the front doors of the elementary school and mom dropped me off with the other five year olds. We were sequestered in a big room. Well, you guessed it. They announced that if your name was called that you were to get in line and follow Miss so and so. I began to cry and did not want to go. I told Jerry to please tell my mom goodbye for me. What a mean, dirty trick for older boys to play on an innocent, trusting and unsuspecting little boy. Obviously, the school officials had so many five year olds that they were dividing the group into classes and each one of us were assigned to follow our new teacher to our new classroom. You will never know how wonderful it felt to see my mom walk through the door and pick me up later in the day.

I was really scared by the whole ordeal. I didn't tell anyone about it but I never forgot it. I've gotten over it but I still have a little chill run down my spine when I enter elementary schools (not really). I moved on, forgave the Simmons boys and Marcus (AKA *Bug*) became one of my closest neighborhood friends.

All of us can relate experiences about when people have *done us wrong*. I can remember telling my parents; *that isn't fair*. In a perfect world no one would ever *deceive, mistreat* or *hurt* anyone else. But unfortunately we do not live in a perfect world and life certainly is not always fair.

One of the hardest things in life to do is *forgive*. It seems to come more easily to children. They *forgive* little conflicts with their siblings and playmates. Within minutes the whole affair is forgotten and they are playing together again. With adults, it is not as simple. The older we get the harder it seems be to *forgive*.

Forgiveness is an act that does as much if not more for the *forgiver* as the *forgiven.*

What does *forgiving* someone who has wronged us do for us? It frees us from the control of the inner hurt they've caused us. Many times people who've mistreated us don't lose three seconds sleep over the whole matter. We may carry it for days, months and yes even years. They forget completely about it, but we relive it over and over again. We are captivated in the prison of our own thoughts. A decision to *forgive*, even though the person may not have asked for *forgiveness*, frees us from the prison of our own hurt feelings and helps us move on with life.

Forgiveness is an essential part of a warm and happy marriage. It was once said that a happy marriage is the union of two *good forgivers*. *Forgiveness* is essential in the work place if we are to get along with people and learn to be content with our jobs. Forgiveness is essential with our neighbors. I once knew of two ladies who didn't speak to each other for over twenty years because one lady's chickens strayed into the garden of the other. What a waste. Twenty years of friendship sacrificed over some chickens and tomatoes. *Forgiveness* is essential on the highway. I know there are bad drivers out there who cut us off and do inconsiderate things. Forgiving at that moment may keep us from saying or doing something we may regret later.

The scriptures teach us that if we want *peace* and God's *forgiveness*, then we must forgive others. It is not easy and it sometimes takes us a while to arrive there. But we are the winners when we *forgive*. We have much to gain when we *forgive* others and much to lose when we do not. So don't stay in the prison of hurt and mistreated feelings. *Forgive early, forgive generously, forgive completely and forgive eternally.* You'll be the WINNER. Remember that old saying: "*To err is human, to forgive is divine.*"

The Verdict

Dr. Roy W. Harris

The Judge focuses the attention of the entire courtroom on the jury box; *has the jury reached a verdict*? The chairperson raises from his chair *yes Your Honor we have. We the jury find the defendant*…….. Many hours of hard work and investigation have led to this moment of anticipation. What will the verdict be?

Have you ever wondered what might be at the heart of many of our problems? The answer might surprise. You may recall the biblical story of Adam and Eve. In the story, a serpent appealed to Eve's pride. *God is not treating you fairly* the serpent (Satan) told her. Her pride said to her; *you deserve more and possessing more will make you happy*. Pride was at the root of man's first problem.

Another word for *pride* is *ego*. In 1 Corinthians 3:21 – 4:7 Paul addresses the root of the problem the Christians had in the city of Corinth located in Asia Minor. The root of their problems was *pride* and *boasting*.

We can learn much from Paul's teaching about *pride* and the *human ego*. Paul compares the human ego to a physical organ in the body. Normally functioning parts of the human body garner little attention yet contribute greatly to its' overall well being and welfare.

When a part of the body becomes injured or dysfunctional, the entire body's attention is drawn to it. The body becomes focused on doing whatever is necessary to meet the needs of its' injured member. The need to satisfy the injured member takes precedence over everything else.

The human ego is intangible, yet no organ impacts the person more. Paul gives a good description in 1 Corinthians 4:6 of man's ego as inflated with much air pumped into it. It is swollen, inflamed, bigger than it should be, and ready to burst.

This dysfunctional organ called ego dominates the focus of the entire person. The human mind, body, and spirit marshal all of its resources in an effort to appease the needs of the ego. The ego's requirements are ever demanding and never fully achievable.

Timothy Keller in his book <u>The Freedom of Self-Forgetfulness</u> does a great job of describing the condition of the human ego. Notice three characteristics present in the human ego.

First, the human ego is **empty**. It is overinflated with nothing at its core. Soren Kierkegaard's book <u>Sickness unto Death</u> says it well; *it is the normal state of the human heart to try to build its own identity around something besides God*. The human ego searches for self-worth, sense of purpose and feeling special.

Man's ego deceives him with illusions that without God he is competent to run his own life, achieve self-worth and find purpose big enough to give life meaning. King Solomon understood this well. *Vanity of vanities; all is vanity* he said in Ecclesiastes 1:2. He enjoyed the high position as king of Israel, great possessions, and any pleasure the world had to offer. He understood through personal experience that man's ego is hollow and empty and can never be fully satisfied. Whatever we try to put in God's place can never be enough. It will always be too small.

The *second characteristic* of man's ego is that it is **painful**. It produces pain because there's something seriously wrong with it. Man's ego produces reoccurring, ongoing, daily pain. It draws attention to itself every day.

Man's ego hurts because it's never completely happy. It is constantly drawing attention to itself. It always makes us think about how we look, what other people are thinking about us and how we are being treated. Our feelings get hurt. Well, it's impossible for feelings to hurt. It is our egos that get hurt because our identity and our sense of self-worth are hurting. It is difficult to make it through a single day without feeling ignored, snubbed, failing to measure up, wondering what others are thinking about us or getting down on ourselves.

There's something wrong with my identity. There is something wrong with my sense of self-worth. All of this causes me pain. There's something wrong with me and that something is *my ego*.

A *third characteristic* of ego is that it is **very busy**. Ego stays incredibly busy trying to fill its emptiness and soothe its pain. Paul gives insight into how ego seeks to remedy this pain and emptiness. He reminds us in first Corinthians 4:6 not to take pride in one person over the other. Man's ego tries to fill the emptiness by *comparing* and *boasting.*

The empty, painful, inward, ego-self requires

validation. It seeks to secure validation by constantly comparing itself to others. Short-lived temporary relief comes but never lasts long. C. S. Lewis in his chapter on pride in Mere Christianity gets it right when he states *Pride gets no pleasure out of having something, only out of having more of it than the next person.*

We are proud of our wealth, positions in life, good looks, talents and etc. We are proud because we have more wealth, a higher position, better looks and more talent when comparing ourselves to others. The empty ego is restocked and the painful need for self-worth, reassurance and value has temporarily been reaffirmed.

This nourished ego quickly becomes hungry again when we come in contact with others who are wealthier, hold higher positions, are better looking or who may be more talented. All pleasure taken in what we had quickly vanishes because in reality we had no pleasure in them at all.

Our egos are extremely busy comparing and measuring others to ourselves hoping to find us better than them. We are desperately trying to bolster our self-esteem, in an effort to fill the emptiness and soothe the pain of inadequacy. Pride is the pleasure of having and being more than the next person!

How do we fill the void and eliminate the pain of our inflated egos? By seeking the approval of others? By accepting ourselves? Neither of these works because meeting the standards of others or own personal standards requires perfection. Therein is the problem. We are fallible and perfection is beyond our reach.

Paul tells the Corinthians that he is not concerned with what they think of him neither is he concerned what he thinks of himself. *My conscience is clear, but that does not make me innocent* he says. The Greek word for *innocent* comes from *the word justify*. This is the same word Paul uses throughout Romans and Galatians. Paul is making the point that justification is beyond his own efforts.

Our empty overinflated ego has it backwards. It requires us to perform a never-ending search for validation seeking *the verdict* that we are important and valuable.

The verdict is in. God has pronounced us valuable and important. The court of heaven has vindicated us. We have been declared innocent, important, and valuable. The one who judges us is the one who vindicated us. Now we perform because of *the verdict* rather than seeking it. Jesus loves and accepts us because we are more valuable to him than the wealth of the whole world.

Our value and self-worth should not depend on having more money than others, looking as good as somebody else, feeling good enough and etc. We should not devalue our self-worth because we are left out, looked over, or look down upon.

The verdict Is In. It's time to embrace *the verdict* and seize our identity, value, importance, and self-worth. We are children of a God who created us, knows us, loves us and we are important to him. Let's live our lives accordingly!

Everyday Labor
Dr. Roy W. Harris

Wow – where did the summer go? I think we all feel that way when the reality of Fall begins to set in with arrival of the Labor Day weekend. The tradition of celebrating Labor Day has a history spanning approximately 120 years. It became an official national holiday in 1894 during President Grover Cleveland's administration. The bill took only six days to make it through both houses of Congress and to the president's desk.

Labor Day

Labor Day has come to symbolize much more in our modern world than its original purpose of recognizing of the dedication and hard work of those whose labor helps make our country strong. Labor Day is the symbolic end of summer to most Tennesseans. This is also the time of year that many sports fans have been waiting for. College football teams in the National Collegiate Athletic Association usually play their first games the week before Labor Day. The National Football League usually play's its first game on the Thursday following Labor Day. Let's not forget another biggie that impacts all of us. To stay in style, Labor Day is the last day when it is permissible to wear white until Memorial Day weekend roles around at the end of May (ha).

In the previous issue of Wilson Living (July/August) I extolled the wonderful benefits of *Vacation Time.* Work also has great value. Work is nothing new and is part of all our lives. We'd rather play than work … or would we. The first mention of work and our involvement in it is found in the very first book of the bible, the book of Genesis (which literally means book of beginnings.) Most of us are familiar with the biblical story of Adam and Eve created by God and placed in the Garden of Eden. We have seen the commercials of Adam being tempted to eat the forbidden apple and the idea that paradise provided freedom from many things including work. If you look at that story a little more closely I think you'll find something very interesting. God provided a wonderful environment in the garden but he assigned man the responsibility to work and take care of it. The bible basically says that God placed Adam in the Garden of Eden not only to enjoy the benefits of paradise but also to work in and take care of the garden.

Spring and summer weather in middle Tennessee seemed to be a bit unusual this year. A warmer than normal winter gave way to a searing hot and dry June followed by a wet July. I was truly amazed when lawns turned brown prematurely and plants, shrubs and small trees struggled to survive. Even more amazing was the transformation the July rains brought with an exceptionally green August. Gardens that seemed to be *doomed in June* not survived but *thrived by the end of July.*

Gardens

My father was big on gardens. I mean that in two ways; big in the sense that he placed great value on planting a garden each year and also big in the size of the gardens he planted each year. Working in the garden was part of growing up in the Harris household for my brother Rick and I. From the initial soil preparation in the spring, keeping the garden free from weeds, to harvesting the vegetables we were all heavily involved. I must admit I didn't look forward to the *sweat equity* we invested in the garden, but I sure did indulge in the *sweet enjoyment* of savoring the ripened fresh first fruits and vegetables from the garden.

Working

There is a certain fulfillment we experience from work that we enjoy. This is not by chance or accident. The bible reminds of this great principle in a number of places. King Solomon tells us that there is no better enjoyment for a person than being able to eat, drink and find fulfillment because of his hard work. He also says that there is internal reward we experience for doing our best. God built within us a need to work. Each person has a role to fill in the function of society. Work is a noble thing and every person's work is important. We tend to assign value based on our evaluation of what jobs seem more important. I think we are missing something when we only look at from that perspective. How would society function without people who are willing to do the hard jobs? Society needs every worker and the jobs they perform. My hat is off to those who do the jobs I cannot do and would hate to be called on to try to do. One final word from the wise guy Solomon, from the fruit of his lips a man is filled with good things as surely as the work of his hands rewards him. When you go to work next week remember that there is value and reward waiting for you. So work hard and enjoy the fruits of your labor and enjoy this wonderful time of the year.

America an Exceptional Nation

Dr. Roy W. Harris

If asked what one thing crosses all walks of life and is essential to the success of every endeavor? What one thing would you choose? Some might choose the great inventions of mankind such as the wheel, electricity, the computer etc. Others might choose philosophy and the compiled knowledge and wisdom of mankind gained over thousands of years. Still others might choose great strides gained through medical discovery and the remedy of certain diseases, which plagued mankind since his beginning.

All of the above are important and all have one thing in common. That one thing is all are successful because they were built on strong foundations. Foundations are crucial in every walk of life.

The term *American Exceptionalism* is not new, but in

recent days has become the topic of renewed discussion and debate. Ian Tyrrell in his blog defines *American Exceptionalism* as *the special character of the United States as a uniquely free nation based upon democratic ideals and personal liberty.* Is America really an exceptional nation? I believe she is.

Why is America an *exceptional nation*? There are many reasons we could allude to, but all flow from one tremendously important one, America's foundation. America's solid foundation consists of three great pillars upon which America was conceived, constructed, and continues until this day. Let's take a minute to look at America's great foundation.

The *first pillar* of America's foundation is the **Declaration of Independence** adopted in Congress on July 4, 1776. The declaration in its entirety is important, but space will not allow time to look at all of it. Let's review a portion.

Declaration of Independence – *When in the Course of human events, it becomes necessary for one people to dissolve the political bands which have connected them with another, and to assume among the powers of the earth, the separate and equal station to which the Laws of Nature and of Nature's God entitle them, a decent respect to the opinions of mankind requires that they should declare the causes which impel them to the separation.*

We hold these truths to be self-evident, that all men are created equal, that they are endowed by their Creator with certain unalienable Rights, that among these are Life, Liberty and the pursuit of Happiness. --That to secure these rights, Governments are instituted among Men, deriving their just powers from the consent of the governed, --That whenever any Form of Government becomes destructive of these ends, it is the Right of the People to alter or to abolish it, and to institute new Government, laying its foundation on such principles and organizing its powers in such form, as to them shall seem most likely to effect their Safety and Happiness. I

The United States of America was born on July 4, 1776 with the adoption of the Declaration of Independence. Why is the Declaration of Independence so important? There are number of reasons, but I'll mention only a few. First of all, our founding fathers believed that God endows all men equally with specific rights. The belief in these rights guided our founding fathers in the creation of the Declaration of Independence, the Constitution of United States, and the Bill of Rights.

The Declaration of Independence spells out three God-given rights - *life, liberty*, and *the pursuit of happiness*. Another way of saying this is every man should be able to live, be free to live as he chooses, and pursue avenues that he believes will bring him happiness. America is *exceptional* because it offers every man and woman an opportunity to pursue his or her hopes and dreams. They are not limited because of who their parents are or where they were born.

The *second great pillar* of America's foundation is the Constitution of the United States. Again, we do not have space for the entire Constitution, but the *Preamble* defines the reason for and purpose of the Constitution.

Preamble to the Constitution –*We the people of the United States, in Order to form a more perfect Union, establish Justice, insure domestic Tranquility, provide for the common defense, promote the general Welfare, and secure the Blessings of Liberty to ourselves and our Posterity, do ordain and establish this Constitution for the United States of America.*

The Constitution provided the framework from which our government was created and has successfully operated for the past 230 plus years. Our form of government is unique in the annals of history. Abraham Lincoln said it well during his Gettysburg address; *it is a government of the people, by the people, and for the people.* The people have the right to change or amend it as they choose. America is *exceptional* because the people of the United States have the final say on how they will be governed and what their laws will be.

The *third great pillar* of America's foundation is the <u>Bill of Rights</u>. The ability to amend the Constitution is found in Article 5. It provides a means to change the document as the governed saw the need. The first 10 amendments to the Constitution are affectionately known as the <u>Bill of Rights</u>. These 10 amendments provide safeguards for our individual freedoms, which make this nation different from any other on the face of the earth now and in all of recorded history.

The Bill of Rights should never be taken lightly and are worthy of reminder in this article.

<u>Bill of Rights</u>

First Amendment - Congress shall make no law respecting an establishment of religion, or prohibiting the free exercise thereof; or abridging the freedom of speech, or of the press, or the right of the people peaceably to assemble, and to petition the Government for a redress of grievances.

Second Amendment - A well-regulated Militia, being necessary to the security of a free State, the right of the people to keep and bear Arms, shall not be infringed.

Third Amendment - No Soldier shall, in time of peace be quartered in any house, without the consent of the Owner; nor in time of war, but in a manner to be prescribed by law.

Fourth Amendment - The right of the people to be secure in their persons, houses, papers, and effects, against unreasonable searches and seizures, shall not be violated, and no Warrants shall issue, but upon probable cause, supported by Oath or affirmation, and particularly describing the place to be searched, and the persons or things to be seized.

Fifth Amendment - No person shall be held to answer for a capital, or otherwise infamous crime, unless on a presentment or indictment of a Grand Jury, except in cases arising in the land or naval forces, or in the Militia, when in actual service in time of War or public danger; nor shall any person be subject for the same offence to be twice put in jeopardy of life or limb; nor shall be compelled in any criminal case to be a witness against himself; nor be deprived of life, liberty, or property, without due process of law; nor shall private property be taken for public use without just compensation.

Sixth Amendment - In all criminal prosecutions, the accused shall enjoy the right to a speedy and public trial, by an impartial jury of the State and district wherein the crime shall have been committed; which district shall have been previously ascertained by law, and to be informed of the nature and cause of the accusation; to be confronted with the witnesses against him; to have compulsory process for obtaining witnesses in his favor; and to have the assistance of counsel for his defense.

Seventh Amendment - In Suits at common law, where the value in controversy shall exceed twenty dollars, the right of trial by jury shall be preserved, and no fact tried by a jury shall be otherwise reexamined in any Court of the United States, than according to the rules of common law.

Eighth Amendment - Excessive bail shall not be required, nor excessive fines imposed, nor cruel and unusual punishments inflicted.

Ninth Amendment - The enumeration in the Constitution of certain rights shall not be construed to deny or disparage others retained by the people.

Tenth Amendment - The powers not delegated to the United States by the Constitution, nor prohibited by it to the States, are reserved to the States respectively, or to the people.

Is America an *exceptional nation*? You bet she is. America may not be perfect, none of us are. One thing is for sure, we should be thankful to live in America where we are afforded *life*, *liberty,* and *the pursuit of happiness* guaranteed in writing.

National Together Way	250.00
International Missions	0.00
Home Missions	200.00
Other Ministries	625.00
West Michigan District	**$ 3,811.61**
State Association	$ 808.94
National Together Way	1,327.67
International Missions	900.00
Home Missions	775.00
Wolverine District	**$ 33,287.05**
State Association	$ 1,753.47
National together Way	2,083.53
International Missions	16,247.22
Home Missions	10,736.42
Other Ministries	2,466.41
Other Ministries	**$ 4,365.61**
Alabama Children's Home	$ 685.00
South Carolina Children's Home	600.00
Free Will Baptist Family Ministries	1,339.90
Free Will Baptist Bible College	1,249.90
Southeastern Free Will Baptist College	326.10
Free Will Baptist Executive Office	100.00
Michigan Church Planting	64.21

The Repeal of Don't Ask Don't Tell

A Veteran's Perspective

First of all it is wonderful to live in a country of liberty and freedom. The opportunity to *worship freely, speak publically* and *put in print* the things we believe in and hold dear are freedoms which shouldn't be taken for granted. We are truly blessed to live in the land of the free and home of the brave. The freedoms we enjoy did not come cheap. Each generation has paid in installments of blood to assure freedom for the next generation. Many have worn the uniform and served with pride and distinction. Not all were called upon to give the full measure of devotion, but many did.

America has the finest, fittest and fanciest equipped military in the world. By design, its' chain of command requires that it receive and follow orders from civilian authorities. The military goes where it's told to go and fights whomever it's told to fight. Politicians are the decision makers. This structure and process have served our country well for 250 plus years.

Seventeen years ago *Don't Ask Don't Tell* became a national policy enacted by the newly elected President Bill Clinton. It opened the door for homosexuals to serve in the military as long as they did not openly *pronounce, practice or promote* their homosexual lifestyle. Congress struck down this policy on December 18th 2010 and President Barak Obama signed the order on December 22nd, 2010. This means that *gays* (homosexual men and lesbian women) can now serve openly in the military.

I speak as one from the previous generation of men and women who have worn the uniform and were proud to serve in time of war. I also speak as one of those who were ready to give their lives if called upon to do so in order to pass the baton of freedom on to this present generation. Edmund Burke (1729 – 1797) once said: "All that is necessary for the triumph of evil is for good men to do nothing". I do not presume to call myself a good man, but I do believe I have an obligation and responsibility as a veteran and an American to do something. That attempt to *do something* is the purpose of this article.

One could argue from *the biblical position* that homosexuality is a sin (and I believe it is.) One could argue from the realm of *the natural order* that homosexuality goes against nature (and I believe it does.) One could argue that homosexual behavior contributes greatly in the *spread of aides* and other sexually transmitted diseases (and I believe it does.) All of these arguments have their places in other contexts, but the purpose of this article is to address the recent repeal of the *Don't Ask Don't Tell* policy.

What impact will open *pronouncement, practice* and *promotion* of the homosexual lifestyle have on the United States Military? It's amazing how politicians seem to thrive on saying and doing what they deem to be *politically correct*. It's also amazing how high sounding words and unproven theories grab the media spotlight only to fade when confronted with reality.

What's wrong with allowing openly gay men and women to serve in the military?

Well, here is one man's opinion. First of all there is **the practical problem**. Serving in the military is much

The Repeal of Don't Ask Don't Tell
A Veteran's Perspective

By Roy W. Harris

First, it's wonderful to live in a country of liberty and freedom. The opportunities to worship freely, speak *publicly,* and *put in print* the things we believe in and hold dear are freedoms which shouldn't be taken for granted. We are blessed to live in the land of the free and home of the brave. The freedoms we enjoy did not come cheap. Each generation has paid in installments of blood to assure freedom for the next generation. Many have worn the uniform and served with pride and distinction. Not all were called upon to give the full measure of devotion, but many did.

America has the finest, fittest, and best equipped military in the world. By design, its chain of command requires that it receive and follow orders from civilian authorities. The military goes where it's told to go and fights whomever it's told to fight. Politicians are the decision makers. This structure and process have served our country well for 250-plus years.

When It Started

Seventeen years ago, *Don't Ask Don't Tell* became a national policy enacted by newly elected President Bill Clinton. It unlocked the door for homosexuals to serve in the military as long as they did not openly *pronounce, practice, or promote* the homosexual lifestyle. Congress struck down this policy on December 18, 2010, and President Barak Obama signed the order on December 22, 2010. This means that *gays* (homosexual men and lesbian women) can now serve openly in the military.

I speak as one from the previous generation who wore the uniform and served proudly in time of war. I also speak as one of those who were ready to give their lives if necessary in order to pass the baton of freedom to this present generation. Edmund Burke (1729 – 1797) said: "All that is necessary for the triumph of evil is for good men to do nothing." While I do not presume to call myself a good man, I do believe I have a responsibility as a veteran and an American to do something. That attempt to *do something* is the purpose of this article.

Where We Are Now

One could argue from *the biblical position* that homosexuality is a sin (and I believe it is.) One could argue from *the natural order* that homosexuality goes against nature (and I believe it does.) One could argue that homosexual behavior contributes greatly to the *spread of AIDS* and other sexually transmitted diseases (and I believe it does.) All these arguments have their places in other contexts, but the purpose of these paragraphs is to address the recent repeal of the *Don't Ask Don't Tell* policy.

What impact will open *pronouncement*, *practice*, and *promotion* of the homosexual lifestyle have on the United States Military? It's amazing how politicians seem to thrive on saying and doing what they deem to be *politically correct*. It's also amazing how high-sounding words and unproven theories grab the media spotlight only to fade when confronted with reality.

What's wrong with allowing openly gay men and women to serve in the military?

One Man's Opinion

The Practical Problem

Here is one man's opinion. First, there is *the practical problem.* Serving in the military is different than sharing a college dorm room (this writer has done both.) Military personnel sleep, shave, shower, dress, march, eat, and a number of other things in close proximity to each other. Cohesion and unity are paramount to fulfilling assigned military missions. One's very life depends on the person next him. Anything that causes suspicion, mistrust, or division can cost lives. Other soldiers in his unit will know the sexual preference of an openly gay person. It will cause problems that only those who've lived in that setting can truly understand. The Washington politicians don't have a clue.

The Public Perception

Second, there is *the public perception.* The image of the military has always been one of *esprit de corps, pride,* and *excellence*. America's military has been feared and respected by our enemies. It represented the best of the best, and an enemy thought twice before confronting it. The acceptance and open practice of homosexuality in the U.S Military will reinforce our enemy's belief that Americans are infidels with low morals. It can and will be used as a recruitment tool by those who want to destroy

America. It will impact the view of the military by people back home.

Can you imagine two men in uniform walking through the mall holding hands or kissing on a street corner? The uniformed image of *macho* men standing tall gives way to visions of a morally declining – morale weak military. This too may serve as a tool, but not for recruitment, it may actually hinder recruitment. Since we now have a professional, all-volunteer military, men and women who hold deep moral objections to the practice of homosexuality may decide to "just say no" to becoming part of a military that permits it.

The Personal Puzzle

Third, there is *the personal puzzle.* This takes on two dynamics. The first dynamic is that the person who comes *out of the closet* and openly declares he or she is gay, will be in a small minority. He will find himself isolated to a certain extent and will be unable to develop essential relationships for the success of the unit. Actions will be looked at through suspicious eyes and sometimes may be misinterpreted. He might suffer physical abuse and emotional ridicule.

The second dynamic of the *personal puzzle* is the *straight* soldiers serving alongside *gays*. They will feel uncomfortable in the up-close-and-personal surroundings of showering, dressing, sleeping, and more that are unavoidable in a military context. What will be demanded of military personnel? Combat, IED explosives, and the pressure and rigors of the battlefield create *unbelievable stress*. Soldiers and sailors sign on knowing the possibility of battlefield stress. But is it fair or practical to require that they live with the *added stress* of those who practice immoral and abhorrent behavior, which they did not sign on for? This could cost more than a decline in morale, it could cost lives.

A number of problems arise from allowing homosexuals to openly serve in the military. We've looked at three. While much more could be said, there it is—one army veteran's opinion on why allowing gays to *pronounce, practice,* and *promote* the homosexual lifestyle in the military is a huge mistake. Only time will reveal just how big this mistake might be.

> **Roy Harris is a Free Will Baptist pastor, national conference speaker, author and journalist.**
> **He served in the U.S. Army during the Viet Nam War.**   roy@royharris.info

October-November 2012

Check Your Vision

Online Edition

Download PDF

iPad and eReader

History Resources

About

Archives

same-sex marriage: OXYMORON

by Roy W. Harris

An oxymoron is a figure of speech in which contradictory or opposite words or concepts are combined. I love oxymorons. We use them often, phrases like *pretty ugly*, *freezer-burn*, *deafening silence*, plastic silverware, *jumbo shrimp*, or one of my favorites—a *definite maybe*.

On the surface, these humorous phrases sound good, but when examined a little more closely, the contradictions become obvious. The most recent oxymoron to gain national attention is the phrase *same-sex marriage*. Same-sex and marriage are definitely opposite, and they contradict each other.

In our day, same-sex marriage is touted as the "new normal." From books and magazines to television shows and radio programs, Americans face a constant barrage of propaganda from proponents of the gay lifestyle. And when the President of the United States was recently described as "The First Gay President" on the cover of Newsweek magazine (in response to his open support for homosexual marriage), biblical truth demanded a response.

We arrived at this crossroads as a result of a gradual decay in the national conscience regarding this issue. It began in 1993 with the *Don't Ask, Don't Tell* policy under President Bill Clinton, which permitted gay men and women to serve in the armed forces as long as they did not proclaim their homosexuality openly. It continued as eight states legalized same-sex marriage. It was promoted further on February 23, 2011, with the U.S. Justice Department decision to no longer enforce the *Defense of Marriage Act*. This vital decision gutted the law by removing federal enforcement prohibiting same-sex marriage.

Same Sex Marriage – An Oxymoron

By Roy W. Harris

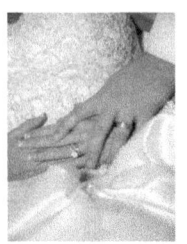

A short version of the definition of Oxymoron is a figure of speech in which contradictory or opposite words or concepts are combined. I love oxymorons. We use them all the time. We use expressions like *pretty ugly, freezer burn, the same only different, deafening silence, plastic silverware, Jumbo Shrimp* and one of my favorites a *definite maybe*. On the surface they sound good but when looked at a little more closely the apparent contradiction becomes obvious. The most recent oxymoron to appear the national stage is *same sex marriage*. *Same sex* and *marriage* are definitely opposite words and that contradict each other.

With our president having been named the first *Gay President* on the cover of a prominent national magazine because of his recent out of the closet support for openly homosexual marriage, biblical truth demands a response from those who hold dear the teachings of scripture. That is the purpose of this article.

We have arrived at this crossroad on *same sex marriage* because of a gradual decay in the national conscience of right and wrong on the matter. It began with the *Don't ask Don't tell* policy of President Bill Clinton on December 21, 1993 permitting gays to serve in the military as long as they did not openly proclaim their homosexuality. It continued its' progress with eight states allowing same sex marriage. It was further promoted with the February 23, 2011 U.S. Justice Department's decision at the order of President Barak Obama to no longer to enforce the *Defense of Marriage Act*. This is important because it gutted the law of the land by removing the federal enforcement prohibiting *same sex marriage*.

This was followed seven months later on September 19, 2011 by the repeal of *don't ask don't tell* allowing homosexuals to openly proclaim and practice their gay lifestyle in the military. I wrote an earlier article from a veteran's perspective on the horrific problems with the policy soon after it was adopted (**http://royharris.info/journalism/current-events/dont-asktell**) which might be worth reviewing. The capstone of this campaign, which undermines the foundation of society, is the recent presidential proclamation of support for a redefining marriage to include members of the same sex.

What is the problem with same sex marriage?

You may wonder why even ask the question. I believe we must be ready with an answer to a world which is being coerced under the banner of political correctness to not only tolerate but also to embrace the homosexual lifestyle and same sex marriage.

There are a number of things wrong with *same sex marriage.* The most obvious to the Christian is that *same sex marriage* violates God's biblical plan for marriage. Genesis 2:24 reminds us that a man is to *leave* his father and his mother, and *cleave* unto his wife: and the two then become one. *Leave* and *cleave* are important words but the word *wife* is the kicker. The word in the original Hebrew is 'ishshah (pronounced ish-shaw').

The word is a *feminine* word and always refers to the female of the species. God's plan for marriage was simple – **one man**, **one woman** not two men or two women. Those who advocate the man to man / woman-to-woman marriage concept are trying to change the marriage plan designed by God Himself. They find themselves in direct conflict with the biblical truth that marriage is between **a man** and **a woman**. God makes it clear that a *MAN* shall *leave* his parents (shall relinquish the old relationship) and *cleave* (be fastened together in new relationship) to his *WIFE*. The two partners here are clear, **male** and **female**.

A second problem is the **sin problem**. Let us not take lightly the admonitions of scripture condemning the homosexual lifestyle. (Lev 18:22; 20:13; Ro 1:24-31; 1 Tim 1:10; Jude 7 to name a few.)

Where do we go from here?

1. First of all we should be encouraged with North Carolina becoming the 30th state to define marriage as being between a *man* and *woman*. Our votes do count! We live in a unique country with the freedom to voice our opinions. We should be actively involved in the political process. We should examine the moral positions of the candidates and measure them against biblical truth. Sometimes we must choose to vote for

the lesser of two evils – but not to vote at all is a vote for whoever is elected.

2. Secondly, we must funnel polls, media propaganda and political correctness through the prism of the Word of God. As I recall, Elisha went against the prevailing word of his day but the power of God prevailed at the end of the day.

3. Thirdly, we must clearly proclaim from our pulpits the biblical origin, design and purpose of marriage and the sin of *homosexuality* and the problems produced with *same sex marriage.*

In my opinion, America is at the most crucial crossroad in her history. I fear that if same sex marriage is accepted by our nation, the 236-year embrace of this nation by our Heavenly Father may be broken. It is time for action! 2 Chronicles 7:14 is an ageless prescription for cure. We must humble ourselves admitting the desperate moral decline of our nation, pray asking for God's help in turning this nation around and examine our personal lives as Christians dealing with any sin the Holy Spirit reveals to us.

If we do that maybe God will turn this nation around and continue to be *awful good* to us (sorry, couldn't resist one more Oxymoron).

The leader of the pack...

By ROY W. HARRISON

O beautiful for spacious skies for amber waves of grain; for purple mountain majesties above the fruited plain! America! America! God shed his grace on thee, and crowned thy good with brotherhood from sea to shining sea.

The opening verse to a beautiful song, America The Beautiful fittingly describes a great American adventure.

It was 6:30 a.m. The hum of eight motorized chariots, manned by seven ministers and one soundman from four states, saw eight men on a mission to discover America. They would do it from the saddles of four Harley Davidsons, two Triumphs and one Yamaha motorcycle. Before this trip of a lifetime was over, 3,900 miles would be ridden and 11 states visited in only 9 days.

The starting gun (revving of the motorcycles) sounded and we were off. We cleared the Tennessee line passing through western Kentucky and southern Illinois. We continued [we]st and the St. Louis Arch, AKA "The [Ga]teway To The West" rose on the horizon. I [was] reminded anew how St. Louis had truly [been] the springboard for the settlement of the [west. Ea]rly next morning, we "saddled um up" and "moved um out." We traveled north through Iowa with corn and soybean fields as far as the eye could see. Truly fruited plains with waves of grain gently pushed across the open plain.

One sharp left turn west into South Dakota and the landscape began to change. Far off in the distance, there they were, the Black Hills! Thoughts of Custer, Crazy Horse, Sitting Bull, and herds of Buffalo came to mind. As we traveled the last mile of the day we saw one of the most memorable images of the trip. A huge lake with a small town nestled warmly beside it, framed by black hills. It was as though God himself had unveiled a portrait just for us.

It was Sunday morning, 7 preachers... You know church was bound to happen. We took time to reflect on God's goodness and thanked Him for the honor of being part of this "trip of a lifetime." Hey, eight men singing hymns of worship and praise didn't sound that bad. With a final prayer for God's protection, we were off. We rode through "Badlands National Park," a maze of tan dunes rising like small glaciers, conjuring up pictures of outlaws and old western movies.

On to Mount Rushmore! We rounded a curve and ascended the mountain and there

The Leader Of The Pack
By Roy W. Harris

"O beautiful for spacious skies for amber waves of grain, for purple mountain majesties above the fruited plain! America! America! God shed his grace on thee; and crowned thy good with brotherhood from sea to shining sea." The opening verse to a beautiful song, <u>America The Beautiful</u> fittingly describes a great American adventure.

It was 6:30 a.m. The hum of eight motorized chariots, manned by seven ministers and one soundman from four states, saw eight men on a mission to discover America. They would do it from the saddles of four Harley Davidsons, two Triumphs and one Yamaha motorcycle. Before this trip of a lifetime was over, 3,900 miles would be ridden and 11 states visited in only 9 days.

The starting gun (revving of the motorcycles) sounded and we were off. We cleared the Tennessee line passing through western Kentucky and southern Illinois. We continued west and the St. Louis Arch, AKA "The Gateway To The West" rose on the horizon. I was reminded anew how St. Louis had truly been the springboard for the settlement of the west.

Early next morning, we "saddled um up" and "moved um out." We traveled north through Iowa with corn and soybean fields as far as the eye could see. Truly fruited plains with waves of grain gently pushed across the open plain. One sharp left turn west into South Dakota and the landscape begin to change. Far off in the distance, there they were, the Black Hills!

Thoughts of Custer, Crazy Horse, Sitting Bull and herds of Buffalo came to mind. As we traveled the last mile of the day we saw one of the most memorable images of the trip. A huge lake with a small town nestled warmly beside it, framed by black hills. It was as though God himself had unveiled a portrait just for us.

It was Sunday morning. 7 preachers….. You know church was bound to happen. We took time to reflect on God's goodness and thanked Him for the honor of being part of this "trip of a lifetime." Hey, eight men singing hymns of worship and praise didn't sound that bad. With a final prayer for God's protection, we were off.

We rode through "Badlands National Park," a maze of tan dunes rising like small glaciers, conjuring up pictures of outlaws and old western movies. On to Mount Rushmore! We rounded a curve and ascended the mountain and there they were; Washington, Jefferson, Lincoln and Teddy Roosevelt. What a marvelous sight of four great men whose courage, fortitude and character had helped build a great nation.

Rain and thirty mile an hour winds greeted us the next morning. Passing through Sturgis, SD, we visited the National Motorcycle Museum. We ate lunch in Deadwood, SD near the spot where Wild Bill Hickok was shot.

After spending the night in Cody, WY we anxiously made our way into Yellowstone National Park. Deer, Elk, Moose and Buffalo were in abundance.

"Old Faithful" the famous geyser erupted right on schedule. Wave after wave of what we'd seen flooded our minds as we spent the night in West Yellowstone, Montana.

Rising early, we rode south through "The Grand Teton National Park." I think I'll always remember those granite Rockies standing tall crowned with bright white caps of snow.

Our "trip of a lifetime" was drawing to a close as we entered Colorado and spent the night in just east of Denver at Byers. Crossing Kansas, we finished our trip the next in Wilson County.

As we rode across America, I was reminded how America is like no other nation in the world. It's mix of majestic mountains, fertile farmlands, lush green hills, sparkling lakes, crystal flowing rivers, multitudes of wildlife and numerous state and national parks make it the most unique and beautiful country in the world. Its history of opportunity is unparalleled in human history. We enjoy one of the highest standards of living in the world. As we gather around our tables on Thanksgiving Day and open our gifts during the holiday season, let's give credit where credit is due. We should take a moment to thank the good Lord for his all-wonderful blessings.

Remember: "America! America! God shed his grace on thee; and crowned thy good with brotherhood from sea to shining sea." We should pray: "God Bless America, land that I love. Stand beside her and guide her, thru the night with a light from above. From the mountains, to the prairies, to the oceans white with foam, God Bless America, my home sweet home." What a joy it was to be the Leader of a great pack on the trip of a lifetime.

America the Great

By ROY HARRIS

The dying coals of thousands of charcoal grills have done their jobs well. The satisfying memories of barbecue chicken, hamburgers, hot dogs and homemade ice cream slowly fade as the warm July sun disappears in the western Tennessee sky. Its dusky dark and the anticipation has been building for hours. The surrounding hills are manned with blankets, lawn chairs and open bed pickup trucks. Excited young artists paint an array of light pictures with glow sticks and fire lit hand held sparklers. A familiar thud summands all eyes skyward. Boom! The sky fills with a rainbow of colors beginning their annual parade across the horizon.

It must be the fourth of July "a date that will live in infamy." Every year it comes and goes just as it has for over 230 years. Why is it important? Should it mean more than just a day off from work or a long holiday weekend?

America is different from all other countries in the world. It is different by design. It began with a belief that we are all created equal in God's eyes. A belief that our Creator afforded us certain irrevocable rights. The right to live, live free and pursue what we believe might make us happy. Those beliefs were so important they were declared so in the second paragraph of the first document that birthed our nation, The Declaration of Independence.

After winning our freedom from Great Britain, our founding fathers saw the wisdom of creating safeguards to protect our rights. They added ten amendments to the newly written constitution called The Bill of Rights. All ten are important. It was not an accident that the first amendment afforded the most fundamental rights held so dear to us all. The first sentence of the first amendment protects a freedom that has molded the moral and spiritual fabric of our nation throughout the generations. Congress shall make no law respecting an establishment of religion, or prohibiting the free exercise thereof.

In 1831 the famous French writer Alex de Tocqueville wanted to find the secret of America's greatness. After looking at America's rivers, harbors, fertile farmland, endless virgin forests, mines, vast commerce, and a host of other natural and educational resources, he came to the conclusion that the secret to America's greatness was not found. He concluded that America is great because America is good, and if America ceased to be good, America will cease to be great.

What makes America good? We enjoy a standard of living far above most of the world. We truly are a blessed people. One reason we are blessed is because of our generosity. Whether earthquake, tornado, hurricane, tsunami, famine or a thousand year flood, Americans are first responders bringing food, shelter, clothing and hope to those who desperately need it. Why do Americans do this? America's goodness shines in these times of need. America's goodness is found in her moral fiber and her sense of decency and fair play. Where does she learn these moral values which seem to automatically kick in during times of crisis and need?

I believe ole Alex was right. The greatness of America is not found in all her wonderful rich resources, though they are many and valuable. America is not great because of her democratic form of government. Though not perfect, most of us wouldn't want to live under any other. America is great because she is good. America is good because of her deeply held convictions of right and wrong and wanting to do the right thing. How does she measure right and wrong and know to do the right thing?

Back to that first amendment, the freedom of worship. America's houses of worship served as her first schools, community meeting halls, polling places and hospitals. They still serve in a multitude of ways to help our communities. Through our houses of worship, responsibilities to God, country and fellow man are clearly and unashamedly proclaimed. Our houses of worship provide a moral barometer to help us weather cultural and economic storms in each generation.

We are blessed to live in a great country which affords so many great freedoms. Our country is great because she is good. Her goodness can be traced... The holy scriptures teach us that "every good gift comes from our heavenly Father who never changes." Our national Pledge of Allegiance reminds us that we are "one nation under God." Our coins and dollars speak to us every day declaring that it is "in God we trust." Our Declaration of Independence reminds us that our concept of freedom as a nation was shaped by the work of our Creator. Let us always be grateful for life, liberty and the pursuit of happiness afforded us in this great nation. If we continue to be a good America we will always be a great America. We can proclaim with confidence and affection those powerful words: "God Bless America." America truly is a GREAT nation!

Roy W. Harris is a marriage seminar and retreat speaker, minister, published author and journalist. He can be contacted by email at roy@royharris.info or visit his website at www.royharris.info

America The Great

By Roy W. Harris

The dying coals of thousands of charcoal grills have done their jobs well. The satisfying memories of barbecue chicken, hamburgers, hot dogs and homemade ice cream slowly fade as the warm July sun disappears in the western Tennessee sky. Its' dusky dark and the anticipation has been building for hours. The surrounding hills are manned with blankets, lawn chairs and open bed pickup trucks. Excited young artists paint an array of light pictures with glow sticks and fire lit hand held sparklers. A familiar thud summands all eyes skyward. Boom! The sky fills with a rainbow of colors making their annual appearance.

It must be the fourth of July "a date that will live in infamy." Every year it comes and goes just as it has for over 230 years. Why is it important? Should it mean more than just a day off from work or a long holiday weekend?

America is different from all other countries in the world. It is different by design. It began with a belief that we are all created equal in God's eyes. A belief that our Creator afforded us certain irreversible rights: The right to live, live free and pursue what we believe might make us happy. Those beliefs were so important they were declared so in the second paragraph of the first document that birthed our nation, The Declaration of Independence.

After winning our freedom from Great Britain, our founding fathers saw the wisdom of creating safeguards to protect our rights. They added ten amendments to the newly written constitution called *The Bill of Rights*. All ten are important. It was not an accident that the first amendment affirmed the most fundamental rights held so dear to us all. The first sentence of the first amendment protects a freedom that has moulded the moral and spiritual fabric of our nation throughout the generations. *Congress shall make no law respecting an establishment of religion, or prohibiting the free exercise thereof.*

In 1831 the famous French writer Alex de Tochqueville wanted to find the secret of America's *greatness*. After looking at America's rivers, harbours, fertile farmland, endless virgin forests, rich mines, vast commerce, and a host of other natural and educational resources, he came to the conclusion that the secret to America's *greatness* was not found in any or all of these. Not until he went into the churches of America did he understand the secret of her genius and power. He concluded that America is *great* because America is *good*, and if America ceased to be *good*, America will cease to be *great*!

What makes America *good*? We enjoy a standard of living far above most of the world. We truly are a blessed people. One reason we are blessed is because of our generosity. Whether earthquake, tornado, hurricane, tsunami, famine or a thousand year flood, Americans are first responders bringing food, shelter, clothing and hope to those who desperately need it. Why do Americans do this? America's *goodness* shines in these times of need. America's *goodness* is found in her *moral* fibre and her sense of *decency* and *fair play*. Where does she learn these moral values that seem to automatically kick in during times of crisis and need?

I believe ole Alex was right. The *greatness* of America is not found in all her wonderful rich resources, though they are many and valuable. America is not *great* because of her democratic form of government. Though not perfect, most of us wouldn't want to live under any other. America is *great* because she is *good*. America is *good* because of her deeply held convictions of right and wrong and wanting to do the right thing. How does she measure right and wrong and know to do the right thing?

Back to that first amendment, the freedom of worship. America's houses of worship served as her first schools, community meeting halls, polling places and hospitals. They still serve in a multitude of ways to help our communities. Through our houses of worship, responsibilities to God, country and fellow man are clearly and unashamedly proclaimed. Our houses of worship provide a moral barometer to help us weather cultural and economic storms in each generation.

We are blessed to live in a *great* country, which affords so many *great* freedoms. Our country is *great* because she is *good*. Her *goodness* can be traced through her churches back to the source of all *goodness*. The Holy Scriptures teaches us "every *good* gift comes from our heavenly Father who never changes."

Our national *Pledge of Allegiance* reminds us that we are *"one nation under God."* Our coins and dollars speak to us each day declaring that it is *"in God we trust."* Our Declaration of Independence reminds us that our concept of freedom as a nation was shaped by the work of our Creator. Let us always be grateful for life, liberty and the pursuit of happiness afforded us in this *great* nation.

If we continue to be *a good America* we will always be a *great America.* We can proclaim with confidence and affection those powerful words: "God Bless America." America truly is a *GREAT* nation*!*

What Cost America

By Roy W. Harris

February 2nd is a special day in the Harris family. It is always easy to remember for three reasons: it's Groundhog Day, my daughter was born on February 2nd and I had successful quadruple bypass surgery. The most important of the three is my daughter's birthday. I well remember being called to my Army company commander's office and being informed that my wife was in labor with our first child. Thanks to the USO and a Trailways bus I was able to see my newborn little girl the next morning. The date of her birth is important - February 2, 1973. The date is not important just because I love my daughter for the joy she's brought to my life since that day, but for another reason. Eleven days before her birth, the Supreme Court of the United States – Roe V Wade that legalized abortion for the first time in America, made a nation changing decision.

Much has changed since 1973. Has America Changed? The United States, once a lending nation is quickly becoming a debtor nation. China, once a feared enemy, has become our chief trading partner and banker. We (the United States) now have a 14 trillion dollar debt. According to the Congressional Budget Office, our Federal Government is projected to spend 1-½ trillion dollars more this year than it will take in. Social Security our safety net for seniors is in serious financial trouble. Many fear it will not be there as more retirees line up for their fair share of that which they worked hard for and deserve.

Our roads, bridges and infrastructure are decaying at an alarming rate are in need of extensive renovation or replacement. Most states are overextended and in danger of insolvency. All and all, our nation is on the verge of financial ruin. We borrow 5 billion dollars each day above what we receive in taxes just to pay the government's bills. The sad thing is that 2 billion (40%) of that 5 billion is used to pay only the interest on what we already owe. It's like maxing out one credit card then taking out another to pay the interest on the first one. The borrowing and debt at some point will become a house of cards and will collapse from its' own weight.

Why are we facing such horrific financial difficulties? The old adage that we are spending more than we are taking in is a given. But I believe there may be another factor, which is not often mentioned. Since 1973 over 52 million unborn babies have been 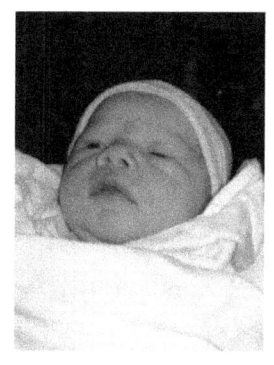 legally aborted in the United States. Have you ever thought about what this may have cost America? In 1940 there were 42 workers who underwrote each person who received monthly Social Security checks. Now (according to Prudential Insurance stats) there are 3.3 workers supporting each recipient. If those 52 million babies had been born, they would be moving along through the cycle of life. For the last 20 years, those 18 and older would be in the work force, earning paychecks, purchasing homes, buying cars, having children of their own and paying taxes. What a difference 52 million more souls would make to our present financial picture. We have and are continuing to literally *murder* our future, one *abortion* at a time.

Besides our financial loss, God only knows what else it has cost us. Maybe the cure for cancer was in the future mind of one of those little ones. New technologies that might have finally released us from the grip of foreign oil slipped through the fingers of the abortion doctor's hands. The voice of a statesman who may have impacted our nation's future and maybe world history will never be heard.

America has another *deficit* to worry about and continues to grow each day. It is a *deficit of blood* –

innocent blood. God's Word is very clear when it comes to destroying the lives of the *innocent*. The *shedding of innocent blood* brings with it the wrath of God. He destroyed the people of Canaan for sacrificing their children to heathen gods. I fear we are participating in similar practices by sacrificing the unborn to our gods of selfishness, convenience, and attempts to cover immoral behavior. In God's eyes, each little one has a face, a name and a soul. They have been robbed of the greatest human right – *the right to LIFE.* The cost is enormous and it could be that American has begun to pay. As we continue to remove one moral landmark after another, I fear the very foundation upon which our republic has rested safely is cracking and is beginning to disintegrate. If we do not return to God's prescription for success, America will become just another sick nation that died in the pages of history.

    The answer to America's future does not lie in exporting more goods, importing less oil or raising more money. The answer is so simple and it can be heard from God Himself: Ps 33:10-12 *The LORD brings the counsel of the nations to nothing; He makes the plans of the peoples of no effect. The counsel of the LORD stands forever, the plans of His heart to all generations. Blessed is the nation whose God is the LORD.* America's future will be impacted by past and present decisions. We have much to account for. As a nation, we owe a debt we cannot pay. Only God can reverse the direction of America. We must beg Him for a little more time and ask Him, through His Holy Spirit, to change America – His way.

Christian-a-phobia

Dr. Roy W. Harris

The recent firestorm of criticism of the reinforcement of the *Federal Religious Freedom Restoration Act* by the legislators of Indiana and Arkansas bring to the forefront a rising problem for Christians in America.

My purpose in penning this article is not to delve into the intricacies of federal or state laws, but to address a rising problem of bias against Christianity in America. Why was there such and *uproar* over the recently enacted state laws designed to protect not only Christians, but Muslims, Buddhists, Jews – IE: all religious faiths?

One factor that figures into this greatly is the changing attitude of the American people towards homosexuality, lesbianism and gay marriage. According to a 2014 survey conducted by Gallop, 55% of Americans now support marriage between two men or two women. **(http://www.gallup.com/poll/169640/sex-marriage-support-reaches-new-high.aspx)**

In 1996 only 27% of Americans believed that same sex-marriages should be recognized as valid with all the rights and privileges of heterosexual couples and 68% felt they should not be recognized. Now 55% believe same sex-marriages should be recognized as valid with only 42% feeling they should not.

What caused this almost unbelievable shift in the attitude of the American people? A number of things loosened a thread, which threatens to unravel the moral fabric of this great nation.

The gradual retreat of the church from its moral space in the culture is part of the problem. Church attendance in America has steadily declined by each generation over the past fifty years. Over half or 55% of those who were born before 1946 attend church weekly. About 26% of those who were born between 1946 and 1964 attend church weekly. FAST FORWARD - only 18% of those who are ages 18 to 34 known as the millennials, attend church weekly.

Agreed that church attendance is not necessarily a measure of spirituality, but it is an indication of the value culture places on spiritual matters. When four of five young adults see little value in church attendance, we should not be surprised when they buy into the immoral teaching of the false gospel of the culture. Eight of ten or 80% of millennials believe that gay couples should be afforded all the rights and benefits of heterosexual couples.

The media invasion of the American family is another major factor in my opinion. The new gospel of *acceptance* and *tolerance* is being preached from morning talk shows to primetime TV. Most cable and major networks have joined the choir in singing the praises of a new moral day in America.

Under the banner of *tolerance* and *acceptance*, immoral behavior or lifestyle should not be criticized by anyone for any reason.

(Space will not permit me to touch on specific immoral behaviors, but I've written a number of articles addressing the biblical and social problems associated with homosexual marriage, homosexuals openly serving in the military, people living together while not married and other important moral topics. These were printed in a number of state and national publications and are available on request at **roy@royharris.info**.)

I want to address what I call *Christian-a-phobia* which is blatantly present in many venues in America. There is a concerted effort to minimize and even expunge any mention of God, Christ, Christianity, Bible, morality and right or wrong from mainstream American life.

Pressure from the LGBT (Lesbian, Gay, Bisexual, Transgender) community seems to have many major corporations such as American Airlines, Levi Strauss, Microsoft, Apple, Wells Fargo, Walmart and others running for cover and away from Judeo-Christian ethic upon which this nation was founded.

Some who embrace the lesbian/homosexual lifestyle toot the horns of *tolerance* and *acceptance*. I too believe in *tolerance* and *acceptance*. The constitution of the United States affords every American the right to believe as he or she chooses. But *tolerance* and *acceptance* must be a two way street. People who are polar opposites in their beliefs must be allowed to express their religious beliefs and live according to their spiritual convictions. Because of *Christian-a-phobia*, Christians are told to keep silent or suffer the wrath of society including the possible loss of their businesses or livelihoods.

Where do we draw the line as Christians? We are being asked to keep our deeply held *Christian convictions* within the walls of the church, our homes and to ourselves. What is a conviction? I developed a definition that has guided me through the years. *Standards are things I live by and could change; Convictions are things I'm willing to die for that will never change.* When we are called upon to compromise our deeply held Biblical convictions, we have no choice in my opinion but to take a strong moral stand.

The line must be drawn when we are asked to compromise on the clear teaching of the Word of God. Should we discriminate against others? Absolutely not! We are to love the sinner and hate the sin. When gays visit our churches, enter of places of business, or move into our neighborhoods we should treat them as sinners who need salvation. We should make them feel welcome, that God loves them, and extend to them God's grace offered through Jesus Christ.

What shouldn't we do? We must not compromise our teaching of the truth of the Word God. Our preaching should address the issues of our day and the culture we live. We cannot in good conscience back up on our preaching when it comes to immorality in any form condemned in God's Word. Even when it impacts extended family of church members. We must show compassion to the sinner while confronting his sin.

We should not participate in or support religious activities such as gay marriages that violate the Word of God. Gay marriage will always be wrong no matter how many times or how loud the government, the gay community, and the media pronounce it to be right!

We must pray for God's divine wisdom and guidance in an ever-darkening world. The war on Christianity is nothing new. Satan tried to kill Christianity before it began by killing its founder Jesus Christ. The world hates Christianity because it hated Him. The one bright light in the sky is the Son of God who will make all things right in the end.

A simple definition of *phobia* is something we're afraid of. Have you thought about what the opposite of *phobia* might be? The Greek work *philia* is a great word that is often contrasted with *phobia*. *Philia* literally means a strong feeling of love or admiration. It is the opposite of *phobia*. It is one of three Greek words translated as love in New Testament. It's our job to do the best we can to turn *Christian-a-phobics* into *Christian-a-philias*.

How can we do this? Jesus reminded us that *by this shall all men know you are my disciples, that you love one another.* Even when we must take strong stands to defend the faith we should exhibit the compassion and thankfulness of forgiven sinners. We can do this by loving both the saint and the sinner.

October, 2012

A Monthly Publication of the Michigan State Association of Free Will Baptists

DON'T FORGET!
October is Pastor Appreciation Month

How Should I Vote?

Roy W. Harris
www.royharris.info

Have you reached the point yet where you are sick and tired of all the negative political commercials? Aren't you going to be glad when November finally comes and we can get this thing behind us and return to some normalcy? Isn't it amazing how elections anymore seem to bring out the worst in people? Regardless of how we wish it might change or be different, I'm still glad we live in a country where we have the right to cast our votes and choose those who govern us. With the next election on the horizon, there are a few questions worth looking at as it approaches.

Should I Vote in the coming election? I could use a portion of this article to extol the personal responsibility that every American should feel towards participating in electing our government officials. But that's a given. I really want to spend my time addressing this question from a little different angle. I am going to take the unusual approach of answering a question by asking another one. *What happens if I don't vote?* I've heard some say they do not like the religious affiliation of the candidates so they don't feel that in good conscious they can vote for any of them. I respect that but I also respectfully disagree. Personally, I do not agree with the religious affiliation of any of the four candidates on the ballot for the two highest offices in the land. But one very important thing to keep in mind is this. Choosing not to vote in a sense is a consensus vote for the status quo saying "it's ok with me if the present administration stays in office or it's ok if that administration is replaced by a newly elected one." If we choose not to vote we have forfeited any legitimate and credible right to complain about who is elected and what direction they may lead the country. Should I vote? When you consider the possible consequences of not voting, the overwhelming answer is *YES*, I should vote.

Who should I vote for? Determining who we should vote for as Christians should not be a hard decision to make. This decision should transcend party identification, the latest poll, how our peers or family members may plan to vote or the suggestions of the media (liberal or conservative.) There should be something stronger guiding our thinking. As Christians the process for determining who we should vote for should be no different than how we decide other courses of action in our lives. The Christian life is not an event, it is a way of life that is governed by biblical principle and guided by a daily walk with

1

How Should I Vote?

By ROY W. HARRIS

Have you reached the point yet where you are sick and tired of all the negative political commercials? Aren't you going to be glad when the November elections finally come and we can get this thing behind us and return to some normalcy? Isn't it amazing how elections anymore seem to bring out the worst in people? Regardless of how we wish it might change or be different, I'm still glad we live in a country where we have the right to cast our votes and choose those who govern us. With the next election on the horizon, there are a few questions worth looking at as it approaches.

Should I Vote in the coming election? I could use a portion of this article to extol the personal responsibility that every American should feel towards participating in electing our government officials. But that's a given. I really want to spend my time addressing this question from a little different angle. I am going to take the unusual approach of answering a question by asking another one. *What happens if I don't vote?* I've heard some say they do not like the religious affiliation of the candidates so they don't feel that in good conscience they can vote for any of them. I respect that but I also respectfully disagree.

How Should I Vote

Dr. Roy W. Harris

Have you reached the point yet where you are sick and tired of all the negative political commercials? Aren't you going to be glad when the November elections finally come and we can get this thing behind us and return to some normalcy? Isn't it amazing how elections anymore seem to bring out the worst in people? Regardless of how we wish it might change or be different, I'm still glad we live in a country where we have the right to cast our votes and choose those who govern us. With the next election on the horizon, there are a few questions worth looking at as it approaches.

Should I Vote in the coming election? I could use a portion of this article to extoll the personal responsibility that every American should feel towards participating in electing our government officials. But that's a given. I really want to spend my time addressing this question from a little different angle. I am going to take the unusual approach of answering a question by asking another one. *What happens if I don't vote?* I've heard some say they do not like the religious affiliation of the candidates so they don't feel that in good conscious they can vote for any of them. I respect that but I also respectfully disagree.

We do not have to agree with the religious affiliation of any of the candidates on the ballet. But one very important thing to keep in mind is this.

Choosing not to vote in a sense is a consensus vote for the status quo saying *it's ok with me if the present administration stays in office* or *it's ok if that administration is replaced by a new one*. If we choose not to vote we have forfeited any legitimate and credible right to complain about who is elected and in what direction they may lead. Should I vote? When you consider the possible consequences of not voting, the overwhelming answer is *YES*, I should vote.

Who should I vote for? Determining whom we should vote for as Christians should not be a hard decision to make. This decision should transcend party identification, the latest poll, how our peers or family members may plan to vote or the suggestions of the media (*liberal* or *conservative*.) There should be something stronger guiding our thinking. As Christians the process for determining whom we should vote for should be no different than how we decide other courses of action in our lives. The Christian life is not an event, it is a way of life that is governed by biblical principle and guided by a daily walk with Christ. We should vote for candidates who give evidence in their lifestyle and stated positions that most closely reflects our own biblical and personally held beliefs.

What specific biblical principles should be considered? It seems thus far in this election cycle that moral issues have somewhat taken a back seat to the economic woes facing our country. Let me quickly say that the economy will ultimately decide the election in my opinion. We cannot continue to spend money we do not have and borrow from countries that have traditionally been our enemies to make up the difference. The national debt is staggering! But I believe there is more at stake here – the heart and soul of America. Most of the greatest nations in past history imploded from within. We are traveling down a slippery slope that could unhinge the moral underpinning that holds this nation together

What should be the role of our churches? For generations the church served as the focal point in most communities. The church was more than just a place of worship. It was the school house, the meeting house, the town hall, the place where folks cast their votes to name a few. Some would argue that the church has no place when it comes to politics and government. I beg to differ! The church should be the light that pierces the darkness of a nation in moral decline. It should travel down every available avenue to proclaim the principles of right and wrong to those inside and outside her walls.

What are some specific things our churches can do? First of all we should encourage folks to register in time to vote. This should be done several weeks before Election Day. We should also begin to encourage folks to make plans weeks before the election to vote. We should make one final appeal and reminder on the Sunday before Election Day. Pastors must be careful not to instruct their parishioners on who to vote for. This would be inappropriate and illegal. That also could endanger the tax exempt status of the church and possibly cause a lot of trouble for the church and the pastor. But they should do all they can to place in the hands of their members publically available information and materials on the moral and political views of those running for public office. They should seek to equip their members with adequate knowledge so they can successfully evaluate those who would govern us.

Some final thoughts to consider. We all should register and exercise our right to vote. We should educate ourselves on the issues and also the positions of the candidates. We should evaluate each candidate using biblical principles and our personal beliefs on the issues. We should pray about whom we should vote for and against based on what we've learned and believe to be true. We should show up on Election Day and cast our votes for the candidate(s) of our choice. We should grant others the right to disagree with us just as we expect others to respect our decisions. Biblically, we are commanded to pray for the winner even if we didn't vote for him or her. This article did not tell you how to vote, but hopefully you've been given some food for thought on what to consider in making that decision. Thanks be to God that you and I live in this great country. See you at the polls.

(Roy is an author, journalist, conference and retreat speaker. Learn more about him at **www.royharris.info**)

How shall we then live?

Dr. Roy W. Harris

As one who loves America, wore her uniform during war time, has seen her majesty while traveling to most of her states and believes that the *great American experiment of democracy* has produced one of the most successful and giving nations in history, it saddens me to make the following statement:

With few exceptions, most of the important areas of our American life are declining. We are literally *decaying* from the inside as a nation.

We celebrate the 40th anniversary in 2016 of Francis Schaeffer's 19th book titled: *How Should We Then Live: The Rise and Decline of Western Thought and Culture.* He accurately predicted the breakdown of any basis for moral absolutes. Unfortunately, we are seeing his predictions come true today.

Where's the evidence?

1. **The Decline of the American Family**:

48%, nearly half, of American children are born to mothers who are not married. 43% of American children live without a father in the home. About 50% of Americans over 18 are married, compared with 72 percent in 1960.

Approximately 50% of marriages end in divorce and the politically correct definition of marriage has broadened far beyond "marriage between one man and one women."

Three out of four women in the U.S. have lived with a partner without being married by the age of 30. This is an increasing trend that suggests cohabitation is now a regular part of family life in the U.S., researchers tell us.

2. The Decline of Education:

Compared with nearly all of American history, the average American school teaches less about important subjects such as American history, English grammar, literature, music, and art.

Instead, schools are teaching much more about "social justice," environmentalism, and sexual orientation.

Most universities have become secular seminaries for the dissemination of leftism and propaganda indoctrination. Students usually learn little about real life and what will help them succeed.

American history is presented as *the history of an immoral nation characterized by slavery, racism, colonialism, imperialism, economic exploitation, and militarism*. America has been the beacon of freedom to mankind and *spent more treasure, spilled more blood, to liberate more people* than any nation in history.

3. The End of Male and Female:

The core of the argument for the redefinition of marriage is *that gender doesn't matter*. Marriage is marriage and *gender means nothing*, the argument goes.

Whether mother and father, two mothers, or two fathers raise children, doesn't matter. A father has nothing unique to offer a child that a mother can't provide and vice versa the politically correct culture tells us.

Why? Gender is regarded as meaningless for the first time in recorded history. Increasingly, gender doesn't exist. One pundit's states *"it's (gender) merely a social identity imposed on children by parents and society based on the biological happenstance of their genitalia."*

4. The End of Right and Wrong:

At least two generations of American young people have been taught that *moral categories* are nothing more than *personal or societal preferences*.

Recently, an incredulous professor of philosophy wrote an Op Ed piece in the New York Times titled "*Why Our Children Don't Think There Are Moral Facts*." He noted; *the Nazis thought killing Jews was right, there is no way to know for sure whether it was wrong*; This sentiment is prevalent among a number of American high-school and college professors and students.

5. The End of Religion:

There are no moral truths in our society because there is no longer a religious basis for morality. A number of mainline denominations have openly accepted gay ministers and gay marriage.

More than the Enlightenment, the *Bible* guided our Founders and Americans' values. Instead of being guided by a code higher than themselves, Americans are taught to rely on their feelings to determine how to behave.

6. **The End of Beauty:**
Just as morality is subjective, so are beauty and excellence. There is no good or bad art or literature. Graffiti is worthy of museum exhibition. Paint thrown by an *artist* from atop a ladder onto a canvas is considered high art and sold for over $100,000,000.

If we acknowledge that American society is in decay, then we have an obligation to do something about it.

What can you do?

1. **Educate yourself.**
God's Word is a *Powerful Resource*. It is living and active, sharper than a two-edged sword, and is a discerner of both the thoughts and intent of the heart Hebrews 4:12 (my paraphrase).

God's Word is a *Potential Restrainer* according to Psalm 119:11. *I have filled my mind with your word so I can recognize sin and stay away from it* (my paraphrase).

2. **Embrace Biblical truth.**
Knowing truth is not enough. Truth must be embraced. There are benefits received by embracing the Word of God.

Do you need **revival?** Psa. 19:7; Do you need **counsel**? Psa. 119:24; Do you need **joy**? Psa. 19:8;

Do you need **encouragement** and **hope**? Rom. 15:4; Do you need **faith**? John 20:31, Rom. 10:17

Do you need **assurance of your salvation**? 1 John 5:13; Do you need help in **overcoming sin**? Psa. 119:11; Do you need to **clean up your life** and be **made holy**? John 17:17; Do you need **help in spiritual warfare?** Eph. 6:17

Do you need **wisdom**? 2 Tim. 3:16; Do you need **direction** and **guidance**? Psa. 119:105

3. **Engage the culture.**

So the question is, what do we do now? How do we find our way out of a rather awkward cultural moment? I believe Christians can and hopefully will focus on a couple of possible approaches in the years to come.

a. **Culture Engagers**

We must engage the culture for the cause of Christ, not run from it because people are worldly. Christ did not call us to *leave the world* - 1 Corinthians 5:10, but rather to *become all things to all men* to engage them with the gospel -1 Corinthians 9:22.

Culture engagers believe we must understand people around us to meaningfully engage them for the cause of Christ.

We must equip our people with the necessary tools needed for wise cultural engagement, and how to remain biblically faithful and culturally engaged at the same time. We need to recognize that *holiness* is *separation from sin*, not *separation from sinners*.

b. **Culture Defenders**

The second approach is *culture defenders*. These

people will take a stand in the political and social arenas on issues that impact the good of humanity. They will stand in the public arena and speak on issues of life, family, and morality.

They will be the *evangelical voice* on important issues where Christians are concerned. They will defend biblical and moral positions, arguing the value of certain things in any culture. These people will participate in important work and start organizations that carry it out and support those who are already involved.

This may be the most difficult work, but religious liberty has to be defended, the greater good must be advanced, and truth exalted.

Culture defenders will be an important part of our future engagement with culture as we move to the new reality of our time. We need more culture defenders and churches that will stand without hesitation or apology for the truth.

How can we cleanse our way as nation? By obeying the Word of God – Psalm 119:9.

Sources Used:

Dennis Prager's article – "*America's Accelerating Decay*" - in the National Review.

David Jeremiah's – "*9 Critical Issues That Threaten the Moral Fabric of Our Society!*"

George Barna's article "*The State of the Bible: 6 Trends for 2014.*"

Ed Stetzer's - *3 Ways Christians Will Address Cultural Issues in the Coming Years.*"

Elizabeth Lopatto – "*Unmarried Couples Living Together is the New U.S. Norm.*"

Francis Schaeffer, Charles Spurgeon, The Gallop Poll, The New York Times and Christianity Today.

A Caregiver's Blind Date

Roy W. Harris, Minister, Published Author, National Conference and Retreat Speaker

By ROY W. HARRIS

When my first wife died almost five years ago, life changed drastically. Although I was very blessed with two fine children, four special grandchildren and a wonderful job pastoring some of the finest people on God's green earth, I'd just lost my beautiful wife and best friend to breast cancer. I was thrust back into the *single world* which I left behind in my teen years. After a time of mourning, my brother's wife was convinced I had been alone long enough. She arranged a blind double date of which I wanted no part. Can you imagine a fifty year old on a blind date? Oh well, I fought it, but what can you do with a persistent sister-in-law? I went on the date and thankfully the invited lady came also. My sister-in-law was right when she prophesied; "if I can get them in the same room together, I believe they'll end up getting married". *She did* and after a year and half of dating, *we did*.

Amy lived in South Carolina and I was a Tennessee boy. We had a decision to make. Amy ended up following her Tennessee Man back to the state he loved. We moved into a home in Smyrna which my first wife and I had built together.

Amy Harris is the program director for Wilson County CASA (Court Appointed Special Advocates) which advocates in court on behalf of neglected and abused children who are in foster care (www.wilsoncountycasa. org). These wonderful caring volunteers are appointed by the judge to help look after the best interests of those precious children.

Now, I'm not the sharpest knife in the drawer, but it became obvious soon after my wife's move from South Carolina that the twice a day twenty-five minute drive to Lebanon and back along with living in another woman's house, was not putting the best foot forward on our newlywed road to marital bliss. So we entertained the possibility of finding a home in Wilson County. Knowing that layout and design of the home is much closer to the female heart than to her husband's, we agreed on a price range we could afford and I turned the *house hunting* quest over to Amy. Our home

A Caregiver's Blind Date
By Roy W. Harris

When my first wife died almost five years ago, life changed drastically. Although I was very blessed with two fine children, four special grandchildren and a wonderful job pastoring some of the finest people on God's green earth, I'd just lost my beautiful wife and best friend to breast cancer. I was thrust back into the *single world*, which I left behind in my teen years. After a time of mourning, my brother's wife was convinced I had been alone long enough. She arranged a blind double date of which I wanted no part. Can you imagine a fifty year old on a blind date? Oh well, I fought it, but what can you do with a persistent sister-in-law? I went on the date and thankfully the invited lady came also. My sister-in-law was right when she prophesied; "if I can get them in the same room together, I believe they'll end up getting married". *She did* and after a year and half of dating, *we did*.

Amy lived in South Carolina and I was a Tennessee boy. We had a decision to make. Amy ended up following her Tennessee Man back to the state he loved. We moved into a home in Smyrna that my first wife and I had built together.

Amy Harris is the program director for Wilson County CASA (Court Appointed Special Advocates), which advocates in court on behalf of neglected and abused children who are in foster care. (**www.wilsoncountycasa.org**) These wonderful caring volunteers are appointed by the judge to help look after the best interests of those precious children. Now, I'm not the sharpest knife in the drawer, but It became obvious soon after my wife's move from South Carolina that the twice a day twenty-five minute drive to Lebanon and back along with living in another woman's house, was not putting the best foot forward on our newlywed road to marital bliss. So we entertained the possibility of finding a home in Wilson County. Knowing that layout and design of the home is much closer to the female heart than to her husband's, we agreed on a price range we could afford and I turned the *house hunting quest* over to Amy. Our home in Smyrna was almost 2,700 square feet and we definitely needed to downsize. The Internet is a wonderful tool. Amy surfed it like a pro and found a number of potential new Harris residences. Working our way through the culling process, we eventually settled on a home located on Castle Height Ave in Lebanon.

    I passed through Lebanon and Wilson County many times on trips to and from parents' home in Cookeville. Never imagine living here. But WOW what a find. We found a new home in well-established nostalgic neighborhood with the floor plan and design that Amy wanted and within our price range. Our home is only a few minutes from her downtown East Main Street office. There was something for me as well. I was able to get two things every man dreams of in a home; a 24 X 44 foot shop out back and an acre of ground. To a man, a house doesn't get much better than that.

We truly have found a wonderful life in Wilson County. My wife is pursuing the professional career she loves and I am able to continue ministering and hopefully impacting lives. I am a writer, published author, national conference and retreat speaker **www.royharris.info** speaking to national audiences and many individual churches. I've been honored to speak in thirty-eight states and also Europe. The short twenty-minute drive from Lebanon to Nashville International Airport makes my national travel easy.

With the peaceful Castle Heights setting and glancing out our back door towards *the back for*ty as we like to call our back lot, I was able to complete a book on *caregiving* titled Caring for the Caregiver. The book was written at the request of many to help those who care for seriously ill family members and also to help pastors, family and friends of *caregivers* better understand how to help and encourage them.

The book is a *Caregiver's Bible* that begins with initial diagnosis of cancer and finishes about a year after my first wife's death. Most chapters end with *Caregiver Principles* designed to help and encourage *caregivers* at each phase in the cycle of life and death. The book was published by Tate Publishing and was released nationally in December 2009. It's available at most of the major online bookstores such as Barnes & Noble, Amazon.com, Books-A-Million and also in about a dozen foreign countries. Copies are available through my personal website at **www.royharris.info** as well.

Amy and I found what were looking for each other and a *wonderful life in Wilson County!*

The Greatest of These - LOVE

By ROY W. HARRIS

Spring is the time of awakening from winter's long sleep and the bursting forth of new life. Just as Robins and Cardinals dance rituals of courtship, something magical happens to human beings. Thoughts of LOVE and marriage march front and center culminating in June with the most weddings of any month.

LOVE is one of our strongest feelings. It impacts each of us. LOVE is not easily defined, yet we know when we experience it. The ancient Greeks used at least three words to describe LOVE. We use only one. Ours is a powerful little word that conveys many different meanings. We *LOVE* homes, vehicles, pets and even favorite foods. We also *LOVE* parents and other family members. These two types of LOVE bring joy and happiness but are very different from each other. We would gladly donate a kidney to one of our children or siblings if it might save a life. We would never make such a sacrifice for a material possession.

There is one more type of LOVE, the tender LOVE between a man and a woman. It is much different and supersedes all other kinds of LOVE. This LOVE motivates men and women to blend their lives together, creating fresh, shared new ones. They willingly choose to surrender individual freedoms and pledge to *LOVE, honor and cherish* each other for long as they both shall live.

LOVE is a feeling. With about half of all marriages ending in divorce, it would probably be wise to remind ourselves that LOVE is more than just a feeling. LOVE must be more than a physical attraction or the excitement of a new relationship.

True LOVE calls for trust, commitment and responsibility. In order to trust, we must allow ourselves to become vulnerable. We place the needs, wants and desires of the other person above our own. Some might say; "well that's fine for the person on the receiving end, but what's in it for me?" Certainly, if only one person is doing all the giving and the other all the taking, that's a prescription for a relationship heading for trouble. But how wonderful a relationship can be when two people work hard at understanding and meeting the needs, wants and desires of each other. Instead of keeping score on what I've done for him or her and comparing that to what he or she has done for me, it becomes a daily passion to think of what I can do to make his or her day a little easier and more enjoyable. We experience one of the greatest feelings in the world when we give to others. The giving attitude should begin with that special someone and not be an afterthought when we've given our best to others.

Trust is the fertile soil upon which LOVE thrives and grows. Trust is more valuable in a relationship than a nice home, new car or large bank account. Once trust is lost, it cannot be easily regained. Even if recovered, the cause of the loss may leave a lasting scar long after it is forgiven. It may never be forgotten. The way we can guard the loss of trust is to never allow ourselves into situations that could result in making bad decisions that could impair or destroy our trustworthiness. Caution is a safer course than risking the loss of something more valuable than gold.

A bad decision made in haste can produce a lifetime of unhappy consequences.

LOVE should also affect our behavior. Some wonderful verses used in many church weddings say it best. LOVE is *patient* and *kind*. LOVE isn't *jealous, loud or boastful*. LOVE shows *humility* and *not pride*. LOVE is *kind* and *not rude or selfish*. LOVE keeps us from *angering easily*. LOVE doesn't *keep score*. LOVE always *protects*, always *trusts*, always *hopes* and always *perseveres*.

One of God's greatest gifts to the human race is LOVE. The scriptures teach us that faith, hope and LOVE are all valuable, but the greatest of the three is *LOVE*. A person is blessed if he or she finds LOVE once in a lifetime. I am fortunate to have found it twice; the first time with Diana my wife of thirty-three years who died after a three year battle with cancer, and a second time with Amy for almost three years now. I can truly say I am a blessed man and that LOVE is the greatest gift one can ever receive.

Roy W. Harris is a marriage seminar and retreat speaker, minister, published author and journalist. He can be contacted by email at roy@royharris.info or visit his website at www.royharris.info

Create a Memory You'll Always Cherish

Have Your Wedding & Reception at The Mill

615-443-6901
www.TheMillatLebanon.com
300 N. Maple St. Lebanon, TN

The Greatest of These – LOVE

Spring is the time of awakening from winter's long sleep and the bursting forth of new life. Just as Robins and Cardinals dance rituals of courtship, something magical happens to human beings. Thoughts of LOVE and marriage march front and center culminating in June with the most weddings of any month.

LOVE is one of our strongest feelings. It impacts each of us. LOVE is not easily defined, yet we know when we experience it. The ancient Greeks used at least three words to describe LOVE. We use only one. Ours is a powerful little word that conveys many different meanings. We LOVE homes, vehicles, pets and even favorite foods. We also LOVE parents and other family members.

These two types of LOVE bring joy and happiness but are very different from each other. We would gladly donate a kidney to one of our children or siblings if it might save a life. We would never make such a sacrifice for a material possession.

There is one more type of LOVE, the tender LOVE between a man and a woman. It is much different and supersedes all other kinds of LOVE. This LOVE motivates men and women to blend their lives together, creating fresh, shared new ones. They willingly choose to surrender individual freedoms and pledge to LOVE, honor and cherish each other for as long as they both shall live.

LOVE is a feeling. With about half of all marriages ending in divorce, it would probably be wise to remind ourselves that LOVE is more than just a feeling. LOVE must be more than a physical attraction or the excitement of a new relationship.

True LOVE calls for trust, commitment and responsibility. In order to trust, we must allow ourselves to become vulnerable. We place the needs, wants and desires of the other person above our own. Some might say; "well that's fine for the person on the receiving end, but what's in it for me?" Certainly, if only one person is doing all the giving and the other all the taking, that's a prescription for a relationship heading for trouble. But how wonderful a relationship can be when two people work hard at understanding and meeting the needs, wants and desires of each other. Instead of keeping score on what I've done for him or her and comparing that to what he or she has done for me, it becomes a daily passion to think of what I can do to make his or her day a little easier and more enjoyable. We experience one of the greatest feelings in the world when we give to others. The giving attitude should begin with that special someone and not be an afterthought when we've given our best to others.

Trust is the fertile soil upon which LOVE thrives and grows. Trust is more valuable in a relationship than a nice home, new car or large bank account. Once trust is lost, it cannot be easily regained. Even if recovered, the cause of the loss may leave a lasting scar long after it is forgiven. It may never be forgotten. One way we can guard the loss of trust is to never allow ourselves into situations that could result in making bad decisions that could impair or destroy or our trustworthiness. Caution is a safer course than risking the loss of something more valuable than gold

A bad decision made in haste can produce a lifetime of unhappy consequences.

LOVE should also affect our behavior. Some wonderful verses used in many church weddings say it best. LOVE is patient and kind. LOVE isn't jealous, loud or boastful. LOVE shows humility and not pride. LOVE is kind and not rude or selfish.

LOVE keeps us from angering easily. LOVE doesn't keep score. LOVE always protects, always trusts, always hopes and always perseveres.

One of God's greatest gifts to the human race is LOVE. The scriptures teach us that faith, hope and LOVE are all valuable, but the greatest of the three is LOVE. A person is blessed if he or she finds LOVE once in a lifetime. I am fortunate to have found it twice; the first time with Diana my wife of thirty-three years who died after a three-year battle with cancer, and a second time with Amy for almost three years now. I can truly say I am a blessed man and that LOVE is the greatest gift one can ever receive.

Roy W. Harris is a marriage seminar and retreat speaker, minister, published author and journalist. He can be contacted by email at roy@royharris.info or visit his website at www.royharris.info.

The Michigan Free Will Baptist
Menorah

April — A Monthly Publication of the Michigan State Association of Free Will Baptists — **2013**

Living Together – Not Married

Dr. Roy W. Harris
905 Castle Heights Ave
Lebanon, TN 37087
Cell: 615.351.1425
Email: Roy@royharris.info
Web: royharris.info

Later today I will counsel with my second couple this week in preparation for their upcoming wedding. This reminded me of something I've wanted to do for some time; address the question of why marriage is important. I do not claim to have all the answers but I do speak as one who has experienced the wonderful joy of being married for a total of 38 years.

Our modern American culture has seemingly declared war on the oldest institution in the history of the world, marriage. It has sought to diminish the importance of marriage and relegate it to the dark closet of the old fashioned and declared it to be out of step with the times. Why address this? According to Michael McManus' book *Marriage Savers*, the problem has become epidemic. The number of couples living together outside of marriage has increased by 1200% since 1960.

There are problems when marriage is not valued.

I've sat in living rooms of couples who were living together while unmarried and heard them say things like; *we don't need a piece of paper to commit to one another for life.* Another statement: *we aren't hurting anyone or it's our business and nobody else's.* A culture which embraces this approach on face value without proof simply has not looked at the facts. *Eight out of ten couples* that live together before marriage will break up either before they marry or at some point after they marry. Couples who live together before marriage and eventually do get married are *50% more likely to divorce* than those who do not. *Only 12%* of couples who begin their relationship with cohabitation end up with a marriage that will last for *10 years*.

What about the statement; *it's nobody else's business and we aren't hurting anyone anyway*? Well, I would beg to disagree! It is….. our business because cohabitation does hurt others. Again the statistics bear this out. Children living in homes where couples are unmarried are *five times* more likely to grow up in *poverty* than those with married parents. These children are *twenty-two times* more likely to be *arrested* and end up *incarcerated*. These children are *three times* more likely to be *expelled* from school and *three times* more likely to end up in *teenage pregnancies*. These children are *ten times* more likely to be *sexually abused* by a stepparent than those growing up in homes with married parents. This lifestyle does impact the lives of others and it should be a concern to all of us. Divorce, child abuse, teenage pregnancy, high school drop outs and career criminals are a few problems that have already arisen from a culture that has sought to diminish the value and importance of marriage.

God has a planned relationship for society.

Reading and following directions usually will provide a better outcome than simply taking all the pieces and trying to make them work with no plan. God supplies the directions on how a society can survive and thrive. He began his instructions with the first institution he created and blessed. God created Adam and helped him understand that he was alone and needed someone to complete and enhance his life (Genesis 2). God reached next to Adam's heart and took a rib and created Eve. He brought her to Adam and blessed their newly established relationship. Have you ever thought about why so many people want church weddings? I believe a key reason is that they want God's blessing on their new life together. God creates men and women to complement each other. They need each other and supply those things which are necessary to find happiness and contentment. God established the paradigm for mankind. A man and a

Living Together – Not Married

Dr. Roy W. Harris

Later today I will counsel with my second couple this week in preparation for their upcoming wedding. This reminded me of something I've wanted to do for some time; address the question of why marriage is important. I do not claim to have all the answers but I do speak as one who has experienced the wonderful joy of being married for a total of 38 years.

Our modern American culture has seemingly declared war on the oldest institution in the history of the world, marriage. It has sought to diminish the importance of marriage and relegate it to the dark closet of the old fashioned and declared it to be out of step with the times. Why address this? According to Michael McManus' book Marriage Savers, the problem has become epidemic. The number of couples living together outside of marriage has increased by 1200% since 1960.

There are problems when marriage is not valued.

I've sat in living rooms of couples who were living together while unmarried and heard them say things like; we don't need a piece of paper to commit to one another for life. Another statement; we aren't hurting anyone or it's our business and nobody else's. A culture that embraces this approach on face value without proof simply has not looked at the facts. Eight out of ten couples that live together before marriage will break up either before they marry or at some point after they marry.

Couples who live together before marriage and eventually do get married are 50% more likely to divorce than those who do not. Only 12% of couples that begin their relationship with cohabitation end up with a marriage that will last for 10 years.

What about the statement; it's nobody else's business and we aren't hurting anyone anyway? Well, I would beg to disagree! It is..... our business because cohabitation does hurt others. Again the statistics bear this out. Children living in homes where couples are unmarried are five times more likely to grow up in poverty than those with married parents. These children are twenty-two times more likely to be arrested and end up incarcerated. These children are three times more likely to be expelled from school and three times more likely to end up in teenage pregnancies. These children are ten times more likely to be sexually abused by a stepparent than those growing up in homes with married parents. This lifestyle does impact the lives of others and it should be a concern to all of us. Divorce, child abuse, teenage pregnancy, high school drop outs and career criminals are a few problems that have already arisen from a culture that has sought to diminish the value and importance of marriage.

God has a planned relationship for society.

Reading and following directions usually will

provide a better outcome than simply taking all the pieces and trying to make them work with no plan. God supplies the directions on how a society can survive and thrive. He began his instructions with the first institution he created and blessed. God created Adam and helped him understand that he was alone and needed someone to complete and enhance his life (Genesis 2). God reached next to Adam's heart and took a rib and created Eve. He brought her to Adam and blessed their newly established relationship. Have you ever thought about why so many people want church weddings? I believe a key reason is that they want God's blessing on their new life together. God creates men and women to complement each other. They need each other and supply those things, which are necessary to find happiness and contentment. God established the paradigm for mankind. A man and a woman are united under God in the institution of marriage. Man is to leave his father and mother and establish a new family of his own. He is to cleave (like glue) to his wife. The man and women become one flesh.

Sexual relationships outside marriage are strictly prohibited and sexual behavior contrary to God's standard is considered to be a sin on the same level with other major sins according to 1 Timothy 1:9-10; (murders, whoremongers, homosexuals, kidnappers, and liars). Departure from God's standard brings spiritual death. 1 Corinthians 6:9; (fornicators, idolaters, adulterers, effeminate, abusers of themselves with mankind will not inherit the kingdom of God.) It is serious business to deviate from God's Plan and produces serious consequences.

Marriage has great benefits.

According to The Case for Marriage, by Dr. Richard Niolon married couples do better financially. They share furniture, food, insurance benefits, cars, etc. When one person becomes ill, loses his or her job, or needs emotional support, the spouse is there to help. Married men are more successful in work as well, getting promoted more often and receiving higher performance appraisals. They also miss work or arrive late less. Married women earn 4% more than their single peers.

Married people live longer. Based on life expectancies, nine of ten married men and women who are alive at age 48 will be alive at 65, while only six of ten single men and eight of ten single women make it to 65. Married men may have better immune systems as well, either from support of a loving wife or her nagging to monitor blood pressure, cholesterol, weight, etc… and may be at less risk to catch colds (Cohen et al.)

Married men are half as likely to commit suicide as single men (Smith, Mercy, and Conn). Married people report lower levels of depression and distress, and 40% say they are very happy with their lives, compared to about 25% in single people. Married people were half as likely to say they were unhappy with their lives.

Who needs marriage? The American society needs it. According to the Word of God, cohabitation (couples living together outside marriage) is sin. It is the sin called fornication. Not a pleasant word and one we do not use or hear very often in our churches much less our culture. But it is sin nonetheless and is devastating to all it touches. Its' tentacles reach far beyond the couples involved. It impacts our homes, our children, our churches, our schools our law enforcement personal, our prisons and more. Marriage is a benefit to society and brings longer, healthier and happier lives to those who participate in it. Let us all do more to exalt the virtues of marriage, admonish the violations and volatility of simply living together. A man shall leave his father and his mother and shall cleave (loyal & unwaveringly) unto his wife: and they shall be one flesh (Genesis 2: 24).

Roy Harris Earns Doctorate

Roy recently completed his PhD work earning his Doctor of Philosophy in Pastoral Ministry from Trinity Theological Seminary. Roy is a veteran Free Will Baptist pastor, having pastored churches in Tennessee, North Carolina, Georgia and Kentucky. He served 16 years on the faculty, staff and administration of Welch College and also served our denomination in many leadership roles on the local, state and national levels. Roy presently serves and has served for several years as Moderator of the Cumberland Association. He is a graduate of Welch College holding a Bachelor of Arts degree in Pastoral

Training & History and a Master of Ministry degree in Pastoral Ministry. Roy ministers to pastors and churches across America and around the globe (www.royharris.info).

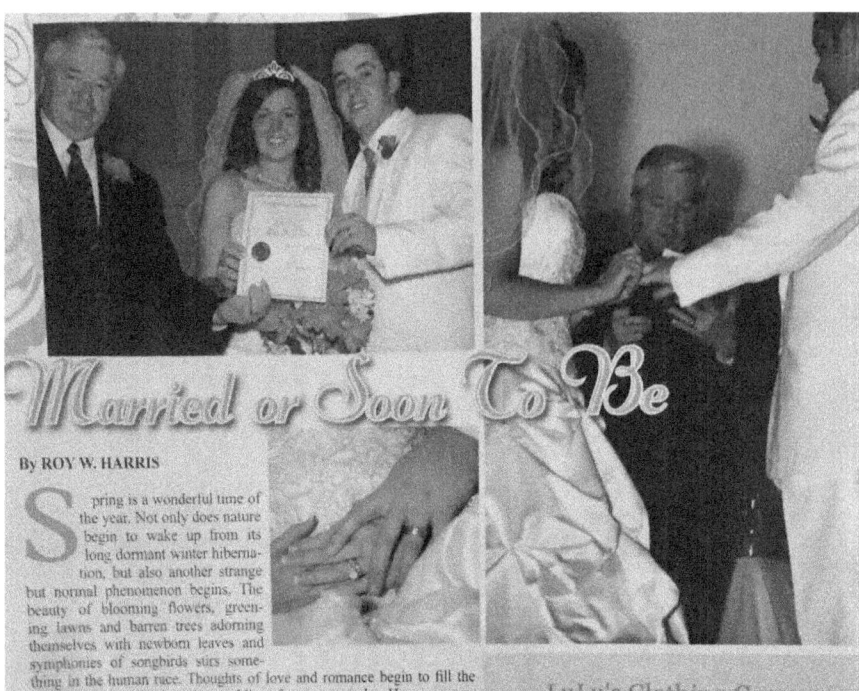

Married or Soon To Be

By ROY W. HARRIS

Spring is a wonderful time of the year. Not only does nature begin to wake up from its long dormant winter hibernation, but also another strange but normal phenomenon begins. The beauty of blooming flowers, greening lawns and barren trees adorning themselves with newborn leaves and symphonies of songbirds stirs something in the human race. Thoughts of love and romance begin to fill the air often culminating in spring weddings for many couples. Have you ever wondered why there are so many weddings in the spring? Spring weddings come from a long line of traditions, which would not be relevant to our modern times. But none the less you can sense that romance and marriage are in the air.

When couples stand before a preacher or a magistrate and pledge themselves to each other, they fully intend for their commitments to be lifelong ones. Tragically about half will end in divorce. There are a number of reasons why this happens, but one that many fail to realize is the huge differences between men and women. Now the physical differences are obvious, and usually the first thing which causes us to be attracted to each other. But there are a few things that are not so obvious. Understanding those differences can make a huge distinction in getting off to a good start in both dating and marriage.

God made men and women different for a purpose, so they could complement each other. They do this by understanding and supplying each other's needs. The Holy Scriptures teaches us that, "It is not good for the man to be alone. I will make a helper suitable for him." Men and women need each other. In order to supply each other's needs, we must first understand what those needs are.

Men should strive to understand the two basic needs of women. The first is the need for security. A man must be present and accounted for in times of crisis. Women need the soft shoulder and strong arms of their men in times of uncertainty and disappointment. Men should be careful not to give the love of their lives reasons to be jealous or feel threatened by other women. A man should compliment his wife daily. A man should always remember he is married to his wife and not his mother, and he should never compare the two (cooking, house cleaning, etc.) After they are married, men should continue to date their wives once a week. You wined and dined her to get her to throw in her lot in life with you, now don't upset things by failing to treat her special. Realize that a prize worth all that effort should

LuLu's Clothing Company

Married or Soon To Be

By Roy W. Harris

Spring is a wonderful time of the year. Not only does nature begin to wake up from its long dormant winter hibernation, but another strange but normal phenomenon begins. The beauty of blooming flowers, greening lawns and barren trees adorning themselves with new born leaves and symphonies of song birds stirs something in the human race. Thoughts of love and romance begin to fill the air often culminating in spring weddings for many couples. Have you ever wondered why there are so many weddings in the spring? Spring weddings come from a long line of traditions that would not be relevant to our modern times. But nonetheless you can sense that romance and marriage are in the air.

When couples stand before a preacher or a magistrate and pledge themselves to each other, they fully intend for their commitments to be lifelong ones. Tragically about half will end in divorce. There are a number of reasons why this happens but one that many fail to realize is the huge difference between men and women. Now the physical differences are obvious and usually the first thing, which causes us to be attracted to each other. But there are a few things that are not so obvious. Understanding those differences can make a huge difference in getting off to a good start in both dating and marriage.

God made men and women different for a purpose, so they could complement each other. They do this by understanding and supplying each other's needs. The Holy Scriptures teach us that, *"It is not good for the man to be alone. I will make a helper suitable for him."* Men and women need each other. In order to supply each other's needs, we must first understand what those needs are.

Men should strive to understand the two *basic needs of women*. The first is the need for *security*. Men must be present and accounted for in times of crisis. Women need the soft shoulder and strong arms of their men in times of uncertainty and disappointment. Men should be careful not to give the love of their lives reasons to be jealous or feel threatened by other women. Men should complement their wives daily. Men should always remember they are married to their wives and not their mothers and they should never compare the two (cooking, house cleaning etc.) After they are married, men should continue to date their wives once a week. You wined and dined her to get her to throw in her lot in life with you, now don't blow it by failing to treat her special.

Realize that a prize worth all that effort should be cherished and not taken for granted. Women need to talk and men should learn to listen. Men should find a time each day to let their wives talk. Remember your wife may have spent all day communicating with a two year old and she is ready to talk with an adult. The second basic need is *homemaking*. I can sense some thinking maybe that is a little old fashioned. Most women want a safe, warm and attractive environment to live and raise their children in. A women's touch makes all the difference in the home.

A wise man will take note of that and aid her efforts. Move the furniture around when she asks. By the way, furniture was never intended to last a lifetime. Honor her request and spring for some new furnishings now and then. If she works outside the home throw a load of laundry in the washer for her. Step up and do the dishes now and then and offer to take your turn bathing the children.

It is also important for women to understand the *two basic needs of men*. The first need involves his *ego*. Ladies, I'm sure that one really caught you by surprise (ha). A wise woman will never tear her husband down at home or criticize or correct him in front of others in public. Subtle nagging at home will slowly eat away at his ego and self-confidence. A wise woman will build her husband up in front of their children. A wise woman will verbally convey to her man that he is the best and he's meeting her needs.

A second basic need of men is *food*. A man's home is his castle. His home is his place of escape from the outside world. This is where he retreats and feels most important. Home is where he can let his guard down and be himself. There is an old saying that probably has some merit to it. *The way to a man's heart is through his stomach.* Men tend to be less understanding and more irritable when they are hungry. A wise woman will not hit her man with the problems of the day as soon as he walks in the door from work. It would be wise to wait until after supper when he's fed and usually more relaxed and his frame of mind has mellowed.

If men and women approach their relationships

with a giving attitude and the idea of understanding and trying to meet the other's need, in most cases the result will be seeing their own needs met as well.

Sound advice for the married and soon to be married: *Developing a good relationship is not a 50/50 proposition as some would have us believe. It requires a 100% effort and commitment by each one.* Relationships built on *giving* and *not taking* are the ones which endure. Seek to be a *giver* and *not a taker* and you might be surprised what you receive in return. Best wishes for a long and happy life together.

How to be MARRIED

From three couples who ought to know

By Dr. Roy W. Harris

What does it take to have a long and happy marriage? I can't think who would be better to ask this question than the people who are doing just that — married couples with vibrant, successful marriages.

So I recently interviewed three couples that have been married for at least 30 years and live in different parts of the country.

Richard and Sandy Atwood – married for 37 years and live in Mt. Juliet, TN. Pastor and wife of the Truth and Grace Church in Mt. Juliet.

Carroll and Diane Culliper – married for 34 years and live in Anderson, IN. The first couple married in my career as a minister.

Tim and Janie Campbell – married for 39 years and live in Conway, AR. Close friends of ours whom I've known for over 25 years.

Here is good advice from 3 great couples.

1. What do you do to have fun?
Richard and Sandy – We love to travel, but I think that you can make fun every day. A saying around our house is "Life's simple pleasures are the best." It may sound trite, but just eating together, watching movies, talking about the books we've read, watching the grandkids, entertaining, having sex… are all ways to add some fun to every day.
Carroll and Diane – Go out to eat, go shopping and take walks together.
Tim and Janie – We love to travel when we get the chance. We challenge each other with computer word games.

2. How do you resolve conflict in your marriage?
Carroll and Diane – We talk out the situation and search the Scriptures to find ways to avoid conflict in the future. We never raise our voices at each other.
Tim and Janie – Over the years, we have learned to let the moment of anger pass for the time being. Then we come back and discuss it. However, we found that the longer we are married the more we learn to value the opinion and advice of each other. I earn to say, "I was wrong and I am sorry." I learn that the truth is good for you, even when you are wrong.
Richard and Sandy – We have fewer conflicts, as we've grown older. For example, we learned that we always get into an argument when we went shopping, so we do less shopping together. We've learned to fight fair by keeping the volume down, not calling each other names, sticking to one issue at a time, and focusing on solving the problem instead of winning the argument.

3. What advice would you give young married couples about money?
Tim and Janie – Watch getting into debt. Live within your means. Don't expect to have everything your parents have in your first few years of marriage. Be content with the things you have and learn to do without unnecessary things. Be generous in your giving and God will take care of you.
Richard and Sandy – Have the attitude that it is our money, not his or hers. Stay out of debt. Have a rainy day fund because it will always rain, washing machines break down, kids need braces, and tires wear out.
Carroll and Diane – Always give the Lord tithe first. Money is no longer mine but ours. This should help prevent a control factor over a spouse. Using the envelope system may help you both see how much money is coming in. You can avoid impulse buying. Beware of credit card debt.

MARCH/APRIL 2015

How to Be Married
From 3 couples who ought to know.

Dr. Roy W. Harris

What does it take to have a long and happy marriage? There is a variety of *how to* resources out there that suggest things you might do to make it happen.

One of the best sources to hear from is married couples that have successful marriages. I recently interviewed three couples that have been married for at least 30 years and live in different parts of America.

- <u>Richard and Sandy Atwood</u> - married for 37 years and live in *Mt. Juliet, TN*. (Pastor and wife of the Truth and Grace Church in Mt. Juliet.)
- Carroll and Diane Cullipher - married for 34 years and live in *Anderson, IN*. (The first couple I married in my career as a minister.)
- *Tim and Janie Campbell* – married for 39 years and live in *Conway, AR.* (Close friends of mine whom I've known for over 25 years.)

Here is *good advice* from 3 *great* couples.

1. What do you do to have fun?

<u>Richard and Sandy</u> – *We love to travel, but we think that you can fun every day. A saying around our house is "Life's simple pleasures are the best." It may sound trite, but just eating together, watching movies,*

talking about the books we've read, watching the grandkids, entertaining, having sex… are all ways to add some fun to every day.

<u>Carroll and Diane</u> - *Go out to eat, go shopping and take walks together.*

<u>Tim and Janie</u> – *We love to travel when we get the chance. We challenge each other with computer word games.*

2. How do you resolve conflict in your marriage?

<u>Carroll and Diane</u> – *We talk out the situation and search the Scriptures to find ways to avoid conflict in the future. We never raise our voices at each other.*

<u>Tim and Janie</u> – *Over the years, we have learned to let the moment of anger pass for the time being. Then we come back and discuss it. However, we found that the longer we are married the more we learn to value the opinion and advice of each other. Learn to say, "I was wrong and I am sorry." Learn that the truth is good for you, even when you are wrong.*

<u>Richard and Sandy</u> – *We have fewer conflicts, as we've grown older. For example, we learned that we always got into an argument when we went shopping, so we do less shopping together. We've learned to fight fair by keeping the volume down, not calling each other names, sticking to one issue at a time, and*

focusing on solving the problem instead of winning the argument.

    3. What advice would you give young married couples about money?

    <u>Tim and Janie</u> – *Watch getting into debt! Live within your means. Don't expect to have everything your parents have in your first few years of marriage. Be content with the things you have and learn to do without unnecessary things. Be generous in your giving and God will take care of you.*

    <u>Richard and Sandy</u> – *Have the attitude that it is our money, not his or hers. Stay out of debt! Have a rainy day fund because it will always rain; washing machines break down, kids need braces, and tires wear out.*

    <u>Carroll and Diane</u> – *Always give the Lord His tithe first. Money is no longer mine but ours. This should help prevent a control factor over a spouse. Using the envelope system may help you both see how much money is coming in so you can avoid impulse buying. Beware of credit cards debt!*

    4. What would you say is the key to a successful marriage?

    <u>Richard and Sandy</u> – *The key for us has been serving God together. Even though we have different personalities, we have values that are alike. The things that we do in our faith; going to church together, praying together, and seeking God's*

wisdom, keep us glued together when our selfishness tries to pull us apart.

<u>Carroll and Diane</u> – *Be honest with each other and don't go to bed angry. The situation may not be completely settled, but tell each other I love you.*

<u>Tim and Janie</u> – *A relationship centered on Christ, good communication, and a servant's heart. Your spouse is a gift from God.*

> 5. What is the #1 piece of advice you would give couples on their wedding day?

<u>Carroll and Diane</u> – *Follow God's Word as to the true example of the husband and wife relationship, and every night when you lay down together, hold hands for a little while.*

<u>Tim and Janie</u> – *Don't expect to live in a perfect marriage. There is no such thing.*

<u>Richard and Sandy</u> - *Don't bother saving the top layer of your cake – it won't taste good in one year. Just kidding! We would say to a couple, "Keep doing the things that made him/her want to marry you."*

Will your marriage last for 30 years? Obviously there are a number of factors that impact marriage longevity. But think about the good advice from these three great couples. They have proven they know how to be happily married. You can have a successful marriage to.

Reflections

Something ABOUT MOMS

By ROY HARRIS

Roy at age 10 with his mom, brother, Jack and a friend

Momisms - I know that is not really a word but we writers have been known to invent new words now and then when we need them. I think you will agree that moms provide us with many sayings that could uniquely come only from mothers. Do you remember some of those momisms? Things like:

I'm doing this for your own good.

Don't put that in your mouth, you don't know where it's been.

If you're too sick to go to school, you're too sick to play.

What did I say the FIRST time? Get up from the front of that TV and go outside and play!

If you don't stop crying, I am going to give you something to cry about!

Clean up your plate, there are starving children in Africa who would love to have those vegetables.

Then there is always the classic, *Always wear clean underwear in case you get in an accident.*

William Ross Wallace said in a poem published in 1865 that *the hand that rocks the cradle is the hand that rules the world.* There is no doubt that a mother's impact on her children shapes the future world those children grow up in and become part of.

There are many great men and women who have attested to the value and importance of their mothers. Probably the most well-known religious leader of our day, Dr. Billy Graham, said that *only God Himself fully appreciates the influence of a Christian mother in the molding of character in her children.*

What makes a good mom then? Good Question! Having never been one I'm sure I'm no expert, but I can say there are some good things our moms did for all of us.

PROVIDER – Moms began providing for us from the moment we began our existence in the womb. Her body went through a transformation that brought multiple risks to her own personal health. She ate for two and provided the nourishment that developed us into full grown babies. After we arrived, she spent the next eighteen plus years providing our physical and emotional needs. It was mom who made sure we had clean socks and underwear and that we didn't leave home dressed like clowns.

PROTECTOR – Moms began protecting us before we were born and keeps on protecting us the rest of their lives. They made us wear our hats and gloves, boots and rain coats and told us when to get in out of the rain. When we got sick they smothered us with VICK's salve, warmed our innards with chicken soup and stood guard by our beds until we were ready to report for duty, back to the schoolyard and playground. They warned us about the wrong kind of friends and sometimes stood toe to toe with the bully down the street.

PREPARER – Moms began preparing us to face the world early. They taught us lessons at home that helped us become successful in life. They taught us how to share. They taught us boundaries. They taught us good table manners. They were homework experts and homework enforcers. They taught us the art of matching clothes, combing our hair, brushing our teeth and putting on exactly the right kinds and amount of makeup. The basics of life were learned from the hands, eyes and words of moms.

PRAYER – Abraham Lincoln once said *I remember my mother's prayers and they have always followed me and clung to me all my life.* Praying mothers produce prayerful children (that quote, is one of mine). Mothers demonstrate unconditional love, compassion, generosity, inclusion, warmth and host of other attributes that also are present with our Heavenly Father. If you grow up in that kind of environment and hear your mother praying for you as a child, there is just something about a mother's prayers that you can never completely get away from. Those prayers follow and speak to you the rest of your life.

We take one day a year to *officially* celebrate motherhood and appreciate our moms. We really should do it much more often. If your mother is still with us, don't miss this great opportunity to show her that you love and appreciate her. Send a card, give her a call and take her out to eat. If your wife is the mother of your children, do something special for her and I don't mean buy her a new mop.

Come to think of it there isn't just *Something About Moms*, there are *Several Things About Moms* that are special and important. Thanks Mom for: *PROVIDING* what I needed, *PREPARING* me to be successful, *PROTECTING* me from all the harm you could and *PRAYING* for me. Your prayers have followed and clung to me all the days of my life.

Something About Moms
By Roy W. Harris

Momisms - I know that is not really a word but we writers have been known to invent new words now and then when we needed them. I think you will agree that moms provide us with many sayings that could uniquely come only from mothers. Do you remember some of those *momisms*? Things like: I'm doing this for your own good. Don't put that in your mouth, you don't know where it's been. If that were a snake, it would have bitten you. Have you done all your homework? If you're too sick to go to school, you're too sick to play. What did I say the FIRST time? Get up from the front of that TV and go outside and play! Turn that racket (music) down! Who do you think you're talking to? One day you'll have a teenager! If you don't stop crying, I am going to give you something to cry about! Clean up your plate, there are starving children in Africa who would love to have those vegetables. Then there is always the classic, *Always wear clean underwear in case you get in an accident.*

Moms are so very important and special. Their role and impact in the life of a nation cannot be underestimated. William Ross Wallace said in a poem published in 1865 that *the hand that rocks the cradle is the hand that rules the world.* The mother's impact on her children shapes the future world those children grow up in and become part of.

There are many great men and women who

have attested to the value and importance of their mothers. Abraham Lincoln said that *all that I am or ever hope to be, I owe to my angel Mother*. George Washington said of his mother; *my mother was the most beautiful woman I ever saw. All I am I owe to my mother. I attribute all my success in life to the moral, intellectual and physical education I received from her*. Probably the most well known religious leader of our day, Dr. Billy Graham, said that *only God Himself fully appreciates the influence of a Christian mother in the molding of character in her children*.

Oprah Winfrey was right when she said that *biology is the least of what makes someone a mother*. What makes a good mom then? Good Question! Having never been one I'm sure I'm no expert, but I can say there are some good things our moms did for all of us.

PROVIDER – our moms began providing for us from the moment we began our existence in the womb. Her body went through a transformation that brought multiple risks to her own personal health. She ate for two and provided the nourishment that developed us into full-grown babies. She provided our entrance into this world risking her own life to give life itself. After we arrived, she spent the next eighteen plus years providing our physical and emotional needs. It was mom who made sure we had clean socks and underwear and that we didn't leave home dressed like clowns.

PROTECTOR – our moms began protecting us before we were born and keeps protecting us the rest of their lives. They took care of us by doing all the right pre-natal things while we were still in the womb to ensure that we'd be born healthy and happy. They made us wear our hats and gloves, boots and rain coats and told us when to get in out of the rain. When we got sick they smothered us with VICK's salve, warmed our innards with chicken soup and stood guard by our beds until we were ready to report for duty back to the schoolyard and playground. They warned us about the wrong kind of friends and sometimes stood toe to toe with the bully down the street. They used gentle persuasion to amend discipline decisions made in stone by dad to lift a *your grounded for the rest of your life,* to only *a couple of weeks.*

PREPARER – moms begin preparing us to face the world early. They taught us lessons at home that helped us become successful in life. They taught us how to share. They taught us boundaries. They taught us how we should talk. They taught us good table manners.   They were homework experts and homework enforcers. They taught us the art of matching clothes, combing our hair, brushing our teeth and putting on exactly the right kinds and amount of makeup if you are a girl. The basics of life were learned from the hands, eyes and words of moms.

PRAY-ER– Abraham Lincoln once said *I remember my mother's prayers and they have always followed me and clung to me all my life.* It has also been said and I believe it to be true, that *a child's first understanding of God comes at his/her mother's knees.* Praying mothers produce prayerful children (that's one of mine). Mothers demonstrate unconditional love, compassion, generosity, inclusion, warmth and host of other attributes that also are present with our Heavenly Father. If you grow up in that kind of environment and hear your mother praying for you as a child, there is just something about a mother's prayers that you can never completely get away from. Those prayers follow and speak to you the rest of your life.

We take one day a year to *officially* celebrate motherhood and appreciate our moms. We really should do in much more often. If your mother is still with us, don't miss this great opportunity show her that you love and appreciate her. Send a card, give her a call and take her out to eat. If your wife is the mother of your children, do something special for her and I don't mean buy her a new mop.

Come to think of it there isn't just *Something About Moms,* there are *Several Things About Moms* that are special and important.

Thanks mom for: *PROVIDING* what I needed, *PREPARING* me to be successful, *PROTECTING* me from all the harm you could and *PRAYING* for me. Your prayers have followed and clung to me all the days of my life. There truly is *Something Special About Moms!*

Calling Faithful Men

Dr. Roy W. Harris

I witnessed my father purchase a farm on a handshake when I was boy. His word was the contract and his handshake was the down payment. No signed contract was needed because his faithfulness had earned the respect and trust of others. There was time in America when a man's word was his bond and his word was enough. There is a tremendous need today for faithful men who are present, trusted, and can be counted on.

How do you recognize faithful men?

Have you heard your voice after you were recorded? It doesn't sound anything like you thought it would. Faithful men come in all shapes and sizes. Some may not be easily seen or recognized but they are faithful men just the same. They wear many hats and march in lock step through life fulfilling a variety of roles simultaneously. What does the resume of faithful men look like?

- Faithful to GOD

The evidence of faithful men is revealed in what they do. But in reality, what men do is impacted greatly by who they are. Becoming a faithful man requires enlisting the help and guidance of a faithful God. Knowing God and serving him is the first and most important role of men. This begins with a personal salvation experience with Jesus Christ and grows into a lifelong relationship with him.

If men are to become successful in fulfilling roles they are called upon to serve in, they should first be faithful to God. God must be placed at the head of the line of importance in their lives. Faithful men understand that all they are or ever hope to be is directly impacted by how seriously they pursue their relationship to God. They recognize their; *time, talent* and *treasure* come from God and are willing to commit them for use in his kingdom. Faithful men reserve *time* for God's *service*, use their *talents* in furthering his *kingdom* and give their *treasure* to support God's *work*. Calling all men – BE FAITHFUL TO GOD.

- Faithful to FAMILY

The greatest gift men can give their families is to love them and keep the promises they made to their wives on their wedding day. Men must be present and accounted for in lives of wives and children. Wives need security in knowing their husbands will be there in times of crisis and need and will rejoice with them in times of success and blessing.

Husbands, you promised to be faithful if your wives become ill. You promised to be there when financial setbacks impact your family. You promised to be present in the bad times as well as the good times. Men, you promised your wives that they could count on you. You promised to be faithful so long as both of you are alive, a life to death commitment. You promised to be faithful to the lady you married and to her alone and no one else.

Men should remember they are setting examples of how children should conduct themselves when they choose mates and establish their families later in life. The apostle Paul said it well in in Ephesian 5:25 *Husbands, you should love your wives like Christ loves the church and be willing to sacrifice your life for your wives if necessary just like he did for the church* (my paraphrase.)

Paul adds in Ephesians 5:28; *husbands should love their wives as much as they love themselves. Because in reality, husbands who love and treat their wives the way they would like to be loved and treated are loving themselves in the correct way* (my paraphrase.) Calling all men - BE FAITHFUL TO YOUR FAMILIES.

- Faithful to CHURCH

Commitment to church will be present on the resume of men who are faithful. Faithfulness to God and family requires faithfulness to the church. Men must be faithful to their churches for a number of reasons. Just as the Scriptures teach that men are to be leaders in their homes, men are to also be leaders in the church. God calls men to lead the church. The church *needs men* who can be *counted on*.

The church should be an *anchor* that faithful men *tether* their lives and families to. Activities of *praise*, *worship, service, friendship building, small group fellowship*, etc. should be a *major part* of faithful men's lives. Faithful *attendance* at regular and special services *encourages* other Christian believers and *imprints* on family members the *value* and *importance* of church involvement.

Faithful men encourage their family members to become involved in church. They understand the need for *reinforcement* of *family values* that are enhanced through Sunday School, life groups and small groups. Faithful men convey church involvement and activities as *necessary* rather than *optional* for them and their families.

Women have stepped in to fill the void left in the absence of faithful men. Many churches would be in *serious trouble* if not for women willing to serve. *Churches need men!* Not just men in general but men *who are* and *will be* faithful in serving the church. Calling all men: BE FAITHFUL TO YOUR CHURCH!

- Faithful on the JOB

The bible elevates work as *honorable* and those who perform it as *virtuous*. Work is part of life and is as old as mankind. According to Genesis 2:15-16 *when man was created, he was placed in the Garden of Eden to work so the garden would produce the food needed for him and his soon to be family* (my paraphrase). Those two verses provide a pattern of *work* and *provision* that mankind was to follow in providing the needs of him and his family.

The bible *frowns* on those who *refuse* to work indicating in 2 Thessalonians 3:10 that *those who are not willing to work should not expect those who are to provide for their needs* (my paraphrase). The bible has something special to say about work when it comes to men. Scripture makes it clear that men have the *responsibility of providing* for the material needs of their families.

Paul is crystal clear in his instructions to young Timothy when he discusses how serious this matter is. I Timothy 5:8 describes *men who fail to provide for their families as men who have dishonored and disowned their faith in Christ. Their fate is worse than those who have never believed in Christ* (my paraphrase).

Men who are *faithful* will work to *find ways* to meet their family's needs. They will faithfully be *on the job* day after day. They will be *on time* and give an *honest day's work* for a day's pay. They will be men who employers will be glad to have in their employment. Calling all men: BE FAITHFUL ON THE JOB!

- Faithful to COMMUNITY

At age nineteen, I received a personal letter from the President of the United States. It was short and to the point. *Greetings, you are hereby ordered to report to Indianapolis, IN for induction into the Armed Forces of the United States*. A war was raging and I was proud to serve my country.

The bible makes it clear that *we have a responsibility to pray for our nation and leaders* (my paraphrase) in 1 Timothy 2:4. Our responsibility to country goes much deeper. Men have unique opportunities in the United States of America. Those *opportunities* come with a *price*. Freedom is not free! It was and is being paid for with the *sacrifice* of brave young men and women.

Men are *responsible* to their country and to *obey* the laws that govern it. They should set *examples* for their wives and children in fulfilling the role of *good citizens*. Men should be faithful in *paying* taxes and *supporting* local, state and national governments as prescribed by law. Now I didn't say men should enjoy it, but men *lead by example*. Wives and children are watching.

Men should *exercise* their right to *vote*. Men who are faithful to their communities have a *vested interest* in who *governs* them and their families. Faithful men *vote* and by doing so *send* strong messages to their families and communities. Calling all men: BE FAITHFUL TO YOUR COMMUNITY!

- Faithful to SELF

Faithfulness to others *requires* men to be faithful to themselves. What does faithfulness to *self-mean*? Faithful men *live* the principles they *believe* in. They *develop* those principles through years of *experience* and *living life*. Men who are successful in the areas mentioned in the categories above, stick to their guns when it comes to what they believe and how they will live.

There are a variety of *beliefs* that *guide* faithful men. Let's look at two. Faithful men live by strong commitments to personal *standards* and *convictions*. You often hear the words *standards* and *convictions* interchanged. Let me suggest a definition for each that I developed that has helped me keep focused. *Standards* are things we determine *to live by* and *may change* from time to time. *Convictions* are things we are committed *to die for* and *never change*.

Faithful men know what they believe and those beliefs *guide* their *thinking* and daily *actions*. Faithful men develop *Godly, biblical,* and *holy* standards and convictions. They *commit* to these as *guides* for living life. *Consistency* in beliefs and actions are the *arms* and *legs* of faithfulness. Calling all men: BE FAITHFUL TO SELF!

- Rewarding Faithful Men

Tremendous rewards are available to men who will be faithful. Men who are faithful to God have the promise that God will be faithful to them. *There is no greater reward than receiving good favor and blessings from the Lord. The greatest reward will be given in heaven* (my paraphrase) according to Matthew 25:23 God will give a compliment and gift to faithful men when they reach heaven when he says *you've done well and been a faithful servant. Because of your faithfulness I'm going to give you far more than you've given me* (my paraphrase).

Faithful men receive the *respect* and *admiration* of their families. Children may look back when they become adults and see a faithful father who *stood firm* on what he believed and *provided* for their every need. The will *remember* his faithfulness and the *example* he left them to *pattern* their lives after. The *love, honor* and *respect* of family are great rewards for faithful men.

Faithful men *earn* a place of *honor* in their churches. The investment of their *time, talent* and *treasure* in local churches earn them *great dividends* through decades of service. Faithfulness garners *appreciation* and *admiration* of the congregation.

Faithful men enjoy the great reward of observing the mighty hand of *God at work* in the lives of the congregation and the *expansion* of the kingdom of God. *Expanding facilities, increased finances* and *future growth* of the congregation are great rewards for faithful men.

Faithful men enjoy *good favor* on the job. Men who will be on the job every day, on time and give an honest days work are in *high demand*. Faithful men receive *promotions* and will always have *the means* to meet their family's needs.

Men who are faithful to their communities will *impact* the world in which they live. Knowing they *gave* back to their communities is a *satisfying reward*.

Faithfulness to self generates *self-respect* and a *good*

conscience. Satisfaction comes to men who are settled in *what* they believe, *how* they will live and are consistent in *living by* those principles. There is a sense of *accomplishment* at the end of each day knowing you've done your *best*.

Faithfulness is a *great virtue*. U*ncertainty* and *instability* characterize the 21st Century World. The world *needs* faithful men. Men, it is time to *stand up* and *be counted*. Your God, family, church, job, community and self are *depending* on you. The voice from heaven is clear. God is CALLING FAITHFUL MEN! Will you answer the call?

The Caregiver Checklist
Dr. Roy W. Harris

Isn't it amazing how bad news seems to come in bunches? In the space of about an hour I received word; that the wife of a good friend of mine suffered a stroke, a young pastor whom I'd had the privilege of performing his wedding was diagnosed with colon cancer and another pastor friend's mother passed away. I was reminded once again of how quickly life can change.

Much has been written to comfort and aid those facing death. These resources may help ease the suffering experienced by those with terminal illnesses. Those individuals deserve all the help and comfort we can give them. Much has also been written to comfort those who have lost loved ones and help with the grieving process. These resources are also needed.

However, one group is often overlooked: the caregivers. Their lives were forever changed after being thrust into the role of caregiving. They are not overlooked intentionally. But by the nature of their role, they are content to stay in the shadow of their loved ones, focused on the needs of the seriously ill or dying. They move quietly through the death process, providing and comforting as they go.

Content to lay aside their own feelings, hurts, wants and needs, they make loved one's waning days as pleasant as possible. These individuals often feel isolated and alone, but they remain strong for the sake of those around them. In spite of their courage, caregivers desperately need encouragement, comfort, appreciation, love, and a helping hand during this difficult time.

Summer is quickly fading. Fall is here with shorter daylight hours and soon the dark months of winter will arrive. This time of year can be more difficult for Caregivers. From one caregiver to another, here are some suggestions that may help you better survive the fall and winter months.

Personal Checklist for Caregivers
- ✓ ***Live life one day at a time***. You cannot relive yesterday and tomorrow will be another today when it arrives. Don't worry about next week, next month or next year. Concentrate on making it through today.
- ✓ ***Take care of your self***. You will be better able to care for you loved one if you first make sure you take proper care of yourself.
- ✓ ***Exercise regularly***. Walk around the block, around the house, around the yard. Find a way to get good physical exercise. Your body needs it and exercise will help you stay sharp mentally also.
- ✓ ***Eat your vegetables***. You might say that sounds like my mother. Caregiving can lead to shortcuts of junk food, sweets, etc. you may save yourself from personal health problems by eating right.
- ✓ ***Get plenty of rest***. Grab a few winks when you can. Work it in while your loved one is sleeping, in therapy etc. Remember you may be up and down several times during the night so there is nothing wrong with napping from time to time during the day. Your body will tell you when you need it. Listen when it speaks to you.
- ✓ ***Find a diversion***. Caregiving many times is a seven-day a week twenty-four hour a day job with no days

off. My diversion became riding a motorcycle. It moved me from the couch to the outdoors. It was amazing how thirty minutes experiencing God's wonderful creation cleared my head, refreshed my mind and renewed my desire to care for my loved one. You may not want to ride a motorcycle, but think of something you really enjoy doing, maybe haven't done in a while and make plans to do it.

- ✓ **Let others help you**. Americans are independent minded. We don't like to burden others with our problems or responsibilities. Believe me, you will need help at some point.
- ✓ **Consider the offers**. When people say: "Please let me know if I can do anything to help," they really do mean it. When you need a helping hand, take them up on their offer. Select someone you trust and let them spell you at your home, the hospital or nursing home from time to time. Remember they will receive a blessing from feeling needed and knowing they've made your life a little easier.
- ✓ **Keep in touch with the outside world**. Caregivers often feel alone and isolated. Contact with others will ease some of the isolation.
- ✓ **Use email, Facebook, texting and your phone** to touch base with family, friends, neighbors, church family etc. Social media is a great way to be reminded that you are not forgotten. Others are thinking about you and your situation and are praying for you.
- ✓ **Watch local and national news**. This will help keep you informed and connected to your community.
- ✓ **Remind yourself that you are not alone**. There are other Caregivers out there. Support groups are available in your community to assist you, spell you, support you, pray for you etc. Explore available resources and see what might best fit you and your

situation. DON'T FACE THIS ALONE!
- ✓ **Lean of your family**. Unfortunately, some people do not have any family members to help them. If you are blessed to have family members who can assist you and are available, take advantage of it. Call on them. Siblings, children, in-laws, and others should help you carry the load of caregiving. Don't be shy about reaching out to family members to help with care, financial support, cleaning, laundry etc. Sharing the load with family members will make you a better caregiver.
- ✓ **Keep your family in the loop**. Communication requires interaction on both ends. Keep your family informed. Let them know what is happening with you and your loved one. Share your encouraging victories and also your setbacks and disappointments.
- ✓ **Trust in your faith**. One of the greatest sources of help and comfort to the Caregiver is faith. Things to remember:
  - The bible teaches that whatever comes our way God intends it for our long-term good and to bring praise and glory to Him.
  - God never sleeps on the job and is on duty twenty-four hours a day, seven days a week, 365 days a year according to *Psalm 121:4*. So if you feel the problem is too large for you to handle day or night, remember He is in lock step with you and just a prayer away.
  - God can be your place of refuge and He will give you the strength you need according to *Psalm 46:1*.

Take it from a fellow Caregiver. There is hope. There is light at the end of the tunnel that seems so dark. God is there and he will help you. When you are lonely or get discouraged, check the checklist. Hopefully it can be source of help and encouragement.

(NOTE: Roy is uniquely qualified to encourage and help caregivers. He was primary caregiver to his terminally ill wife for three years before she passed away from complications of breast cancer. His book <u>Caring for the Caregiver</u> is a great resource and is available in over 30 countries around the world. The book may be purchased online through Amazon, Barnes and Noble etc. or for a signed copy or more caregiver information email Roy. **roy@royharris.info**.)

HEARD THE NEWS?

BY ROY W. HARRIS

The excitement was high as the moving truck backed into the driveway. The new minister and his family had arrived. The next Sunday, the preacher stepped to the platform, Bible in hand and pastoral gun loaded with an inaugural sermon. Hopes were high as he took the helm of the local ship of Zion.

Fast forward a few years. The minister drags slowly toward the pulpit. Head down, his sad countenance and demeanor telegraph that something is wrong. He slips his hand inside his suit coat and unfolds a neatly creased paper and begins to read. As he completes his resignation, the stunned congregation sits in silence. Some begin to cry. Others cannot believe what just happened, and most are simply numb from shock. A few days later, a moving truck pulls out of the driveway, and the local ship of Zion sends out a distress call for a new minister to take the helm.

Unfortunately, this scene is repeated countless times in the lives of pastors and churches. Why do pastors not stay longer? Why do they leave the ministry at such an alarming rate? Consider a few suggestions to help churches keep good pastors and to help pastors enjoy longer tenure in churches.

Heard The News?

Dr. Roy W. Harris

The excitement was high as the moving truck backed into the driveway. The new minister and his family had arrived! The preacher mounts the stage, Bible in hand and pastoral gun loaded with his inaugural sermon. Hopes are high as he takes the helm of the local ship of Zion.

Fast-forward a few years. The minister slowly moves toward the podium. Head down, his sad countenance and demeanor telegraph that something is wrong. He slips his hand inside his suit coat and unfolds a neatly creased paper and begins to read. As he completes the announcement of his resignation, the congregation is stunned and sits in silence. Some begin sobbing. Others cannot believe what just happened and most are simply numb from shock of what has just coursed its' way through the building. The moving truck pulls out of the driveway and the local ship of Zion again sends out a distress call for a new minister to man the helm.

Unfortunately this scene is repeated countless times in the lives of our pastors and churches. Why do our pastors not stay longer? Why are ministers leaving the ministry at an alarming rate? Much could be said to address these two questions but the purpose of this article is to offer suggestions on how churches can keep good pastors and how pastors can enjoy longer tenure in churches. The article makes suggestions for both.

How to keep your Pastor longer?

Many churches have become accustomed to losing their pastors after a few years often never stopping to ask; *is there anything we can do to keep our pastors longer?* Here are 10 brief suggestions.

1. **Birthday** - Remember and do something special for your pastor on his birthday. Announce it ahead of time behind his back. Schedule a time of celebration, prepare a special cake and encourage each church family to bring a card and a small gift of appreciation.
2. **Appreciation Sunday** – Designate an annual Sunday each year to show your appreciation for your pastor. Don't be *chintzy*! Be creative. Do something different each year to truly surprise him and show that you appreciate him. An all-expense paid weekend with a Sunday off for him and his wife. A new IPAD or laptop computer. The appreciation gifts should increase in value year by year.
3. **Christmas Bonus** – A week's salary is a good place to start. The annual Christmas program is a good time to present it to him. Many pastor churches far from home and the extra money comes in handy as they travel back to their homes to spend time with family for Christmas.
4. **Anniversary with the church**- Recognize those special anniversaries of the pastor assuming the helm of the church. 1, 5, 10, 15, 20 years and etc. are all special anniversaries of service to the church and deserve special recognition. The pastor probably has worn out at least 5 cars serving the church if he's been there for 20 years or more. Consider purchasing him a new car and present it to

him on that special anniversary. (Keep the smelling sauce handy.)
5. **Seniority** – Recognize the cumulative years of service of your pastor. If your new pastor has already served many years in the ministry, don't treat him as if he had just begun in the ministry. Here's an idea. Add another line or two to your church constitution/bi-laws basing weeks of vacation on years in the ministry instead of years with the church. Extend to him this similar employment benefit that many church members enjoy.
6. **Vacation** – have an understanding with your pastor that when he leaves on vacation that others IE deacons/church leaders will handle all church matters until he returns. Church members must be *trained* to resist the urge to call the pastor when he and his family are away for a much needed vacation.
7. **Day Off** – Encourage your pastor to designate and take a day off. Reinforce it with the church family. Most church members get two days off each week. Make sure your pastor gets at least one.
8. **Conferences/Conventions** – Pastor's need encouragement, fresh ideas and also to have their personal batteries recharged from time to time. Send your pastor to the State Meeting and National Convention. Cover his travel, lodging and meals (include his wife's meals also). He will be around fellow ministers, hear messages that will encourage him, attend seminar/workshops that may spark new ideas to help your church and he will represent your church's interest on the state and national levels
9. **Retirement** – Talk with your pastor about his retirement. Set aside money in his financial package for his retirement. The Free Will Baptist Board of Retirement has a great program to consider.

10. **Raise** – Give a small raise *every year*. Not giving a raise sends the wrong signal to pastors.

How to stay longer at your church?
1. **Ask the right questions** before committing to the new church. Ask for a copy of the church's Constitution/bi-laws and budget before you agree to visit/candidate for the church. You can find out a great deal about the church and its attitude and care for the pastor by looking closely at these documents.
2. **Begin the relationship on the same page** with the church on the issues that will directly impact you and your family. Be open, honest and up front.
3. **Take a day off each week**. Do it *religiously*. Consider another day besides Monday; you'll enjoy your day off more.
4. **Exercise Regularly**. This is a great way to relieve stress and keep your good health.
5. **Find something you enjoy** and do it regularly! It is not a sin to have fun and enjoy life. It will provide a great diversion and let the pastor's mind rest from church problems and issues.
6. **Designate one evening per week as family night** and try not to let anything interfere with it. Friday nights worked well for us. Do things the kids enjoy and want to do. Chucky Cheese, Bowling and a Theme Park are a few ideas.
7. **Never stop dating your wife.** Call her up and ask her for a date. Email her a *mushy* note. Pick up her favorite candy bar or a rose at the gas station for no reason. Make her feel even more special now than the day you married her. She'll be happier and you will be too.
8. **Prioritize and attend your children's special**

events and activities. Be present and accounted for at ball games, school plays, PTA meetings and etc. The pastor's children may not remember every event he attends, but they will certainly remember the important ones he missed.

9. **Attend the National Convention, State Meeting** and at least one other conference or seminar each year. This will help keep you refreshed and encouraged. It may provide the lift many times needed to continue the good fight in the ministry.
10. **Fellowship with other pastors.** Take the initiative. Find a pastor friend in the area and meet for lunch a couple of times a month. Pastors can share *pastoral stuff* with another preacher that cannot be shared with his wife or laymen.

Final Thoughts

Churches – Churches whose pastors have a long tenure tend to thrive. The stability of not entertaining the thought that the pastor might be leaving brings a comfort and calm to congregation. The 2 – 4 year pastoral revolving door of pastoral change doesn't have to be permanent. Churches generally love and appreciate their pastors. It is important to be discerning of those things that are important to pastors and be creative in ways to let them know those things are important to the church also.

Pastors – Pastors should remember that the longer they stay at a church, generally the more effective they become. Taking care of one's personal, spiritual, emotional, family and physical needs are paramount if the pastor is to endure and continue to make an impact for the church and the kingdom.

Instead of hearing the news that another pastor has resigned, we can spread the news that we want our pastors to stay longer.

Missions in the news...

Burkes express thanks for prayer, financial support

This is it!! By the time you read this article, we will have had our first preview service!! It's hard to believe how time has flown as we have prepared for this service! Our core group is very excited and we have had multiple meetings to plug our folks into their areas of ministry. We have spent the last month preparing the theatre for services. Thank you to all of you who have supported our work here, as the last few months have been very expensive. The costs of "setting up shop" are pretty heavy! But, how do you put a price tag on changed lives? This is why we are here! Pray with us that God will use us to find the many lost coins here in Castle Rock. We hope that many of the folks who have not joined us for our Bible studies will visit with us during these preview services. We would like to add three orfour more families to our core group during the next few months. Our church needs to be able to offer nursery, toddler's church, and children's church when we launch, as well as the adult worship service needs. As you know, this takes a good group of workers to pull off! We have most of the places filled, but we still need a few more helpers.

We are also thankful for the many new friends that have been made during the church planting process—not just among our core group, but in our community as well. Susan has also been able to start helping at one of the local elementary schools as a volunteer Spanish interpreter. We are praying that her contacts will lead to Spanish services at our church.

Thank you for keeping us in the Acts 1:8 budget for this new year. We know that tough financial times have forced many cutbacks in the state budget, and we are grateful to be kept in the plan. We will do our very best to be worthy of your support as we work hard to build Truth Free Will Baptist Church here in Castle Rock. Please make sure to visit our website when you get a chance. Truthfwb.com

May God bless you in your work for Him!
Donnie Burke and Family

Susan and Donnie Burke

Brandon, Tyler and Katie Burke

Criticism — Who needs it?

By Roy W. Harris

Criticism is part of life. It may come from those who love us most or those who may not even like us. It may arrive like cold water poured on the flames of a great success or like stinging salt in the open wound of a setback. Have you ever seen a name pop up on your Caller ID and think; "oh no, what is it this time?" It almost seems that some people have the *gift* of criticism and feel they should *exercise* it at every opportunity.

Regardless of whether it is justified or not, receiving criticism is not normally a pleasant experience. How should we respond when we are criticized? Criticism offered with the right attitude and done in the right way can be a good thing. Criticism, when done in a constructive way to help us, may actually suggest ways to save us problems and create better situations for us.

While serving in my first pastorate, our church was growing and we desperately needed more room. Our church had a pre-school and we were in the process of expanding into a full-blown Christian school. We formed the appropriate committees and made plans to construct a new educational building and cafeteria/fellowship hall. One committee member failed to attend any planning sessions and showed up at the final session shortly before the plans were to be presented to the church. After he'd looked over the plans, I asked him; "how do you like the plans?" He responded; "I don't." My young pastoral fervor got the best of me and I snapped back; "what don't you like about them?" It upset me that he failed to attend a single planning session and now he wanted to criticize the committee's work. He then showed me a major flaw in the plans. The restrooms were where the offices needed to be and vise/versa. He was absolutely right. We changed the plans and built the new building. I learned a valuable lesson from that experience about the value of criticism.

In Exodus chapter eighteen Moses' father-in-law Jethro brings Moses' wife and two sons to join him on his journey to the promise land. After a great time of celebration, Jethro observes Moses handling his daily leadership responsibilities. He correctly discerns that Moses is trying to do too much and will burn out quickly if something doesn't change. He truly has Moses and the children of Israel's welfare at heart. Jethro first offers the criticism in verse 14 (Roy's paraphrase) Moses' father-in-law saw all that he was trying to do and ask if he realized what he was doing to these people. He goes on to tell Moses in verse seventeen that what he was trying to do was not good. He then offers Moses a suggestion to help make the situation better. In verse 21 he encourages Moses to choose good qualified men to handle the small matters and save himself for the major issues that faced the people. Moses's response provides us with a great step-by-step way of handling criticism.

Below are *four simple steps* which may be helpful as you are confronted with criticism.

Step 1 - LISTEN to it. Moses heard Jethro out. Have you been introduced to someone you didn't know and became so busy thinking about what you should say and shaking the person's hand that you totally missed the person's name? A similar thing can happen when we hear criticism. We sometimes throw up barriers because of who is delivering the criticism or simply because we are being criticized. We need to hold our tongues and *listen* to the details of the criticism before we *speak*. This does two things: 1. It helps us gain a better understanding of what we are dealing with and 2. It provides an opportunity for others to be heard. Even if we choose not to respond in the way others feel we should, they will feel that they've had a hearing. Many times just letting folks get it off their chests is all that is needed.

Step 2 - LOOK at it. Moses looked at the details of the plan Jethro had suggested. Once you've heard the criticism, thank the person for bringing it to your attention and tell them that you will certainly give it some thought. Then seriously examine the criticism/suggestion. Look at the merits of the criticism. Is this a valid criticism? Is there a problem that should be addressed? Are there changes which should be made? Is this person's suggestion the right way to go? You will then know if you should accept or reject the criticism.

Step 3 - LEARN from it. Moses recognized that Jethro was right and implemented his suggestions. If you determine the criticism to be a valid one and the suggestions for change good ones, then don't let your pride hinder you from doing what your *gut* tells you that you should. Make the changes. Move in another direction. Implement a new procedure. Stop this or start that. We never reach the place that we cannot learn from others.

Step 4 - LIVE above it. After you've *LISTENED* to it, *LOOKED* at it, *LEARNED* from it and the criticism is unjust or not valid, what should you do? Choose simply to *LIVE* above it. Sometimes the best response is not to respond at all. Do not spend a great deal of time rehashing the matter. Move on with life. File the criticism in the back of your mental filing cabinet and leave it there. Take the *high road* and continue doing what you're doing.

CRITICISM – Who Needs It? Criticism is part of life. It will come in times of great success and also great disappointment. It can be valid but it can also be bogus. It can be helpful and also hurtful. However it may come, we should do our best to handle it well.

Criticism – Who Needs It?

By Roy W. Harris

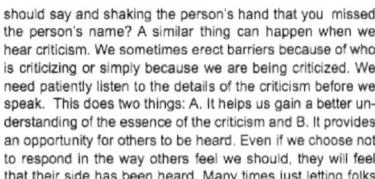

Criticism is part of life. It may come from those who love us or those who may not even like us. It may be constructive or debilitating. Have you ever seen a name pop up on your Caller ID and think; "oh no, what is it this time?" It almost seems that some people have the gift of criticism and feel they should exercise it at every opportunity.

Whether it is justified or not, receiving criticism is usually not a pleasant experience. How should we respond when we are criticized? Criticism can be beneficial when offered with the correct attitude and done in the right way. Constructive Criticism may suggest ways to solve problems and create better atmosphere.

While serving in my first pastorate, our church was growing and we desperately needed more room. We had a preschool and we were in the process of expanding into a K- 12 Christian school. We formed appropriate committees and made plans to construct a new educational building and cafeteria/fellowship hall. However, one committee member failed to attend any planning sessions until the final meeting shortly before the plans were to be presented to the church. After he had looked over the plans, I asked him how he liked the them? He responded; "I don't." My young pastoral ire took over and I snapped back; "What don't you like about them?" It upset me that he failed to attend a single planning session and now he wanted to criticize the committee's work. He then showed me a major flaw in the plans. The rest rooms were where the offices needed to be. He was absolutely right. We changed the plans and built the new building. I learned a valuable lesson about the value of criticism from that experience.

In Exodus eighteen Moses' father-in-law Jethro brings Moses' wife and two sons to join him on his journey to the promise land. After a great time of celebration, Jethro observes Moses handling his daily leadership responsibilities. He correctly discerns that Moses is trying to do too much and will burn out quickly if something doesn't change. He truly has Moses and the children of Israel's welfare at heart. Jethro first offers the criticism in verse 14. He saw all that the problems he was dealing with and asked Moses if he realized what he was doing to the people. He told Moses that what he was doing was not good and then offered a suggestion to make the situation better. In verse 21 he encourages Moses to choose qualified men to handle the small matters and save himself for the major issues that the people faced. Moses' response provides us with a great step by step way of handling criticism.

Below are four simple steps which may be helpful as you are confronted with criticism.

LISTEN

Moses listened to Jethro. Have you been introduced to someone and became so busy thinking about what you should say and shaking the person's hand that you missed the person's name? A similar thing can happen when we hear criticism. We sometimes erect barriers because of who is criticizing or simply because we are being criticized. We need patiently listen to the details of the criticism before we speak. This does two things: A. It helps us gain a better understanding of the essence of the criticism and B. It provides an opportunity for others to be heard. Even if we choose not to respond in the way others feel we should, they will feel that their side has been heard. Many times just letting folks state their opinion is all that is needed.

LOOK

Moses looked at the details of the Jethro's plan. Once you have heard the criticism, thank the person for bringing it to your attention and tell them that you will consider their viewpoint. Then, seriously examine what they have said and look at the merits of the criticism. Is it a valid criticism? Is there a problem that should be addressed? Are there changes that should be made? Is this person's offering a better alternative or direction? You will then know if you should accept or reject the criticism.

LEARN

Moses recognized that Jethro was right and implemented his suggestions. If the criticism is valid then don't let pride hinder you making adjustments. Make the changes. Move in another direction. Implement a new procedure. Stop this plan of action or start an alternative plan. We can always learn from others.

LIVE

After you've LISTENED to it, LOOKED at it, LEARNED and the criticism is not warranted, what should you do? Choose to simply to LIVE above it. Sometimes the best response is no response at all. Do not spend a great deal of time rehashing the matter. Move on with life. File the criticism in the back of your mind and leave it there. Take the high road and continue doing what you're doing.

Criticism. Who Needs It? Criticism is part of life. It will come in times of success and disappointment. It can be valid but it can also be unreasonable. It can be helpful or hurtful. However it may come, we should do our best to handle it well.

Roy Harris is a Free Will Baptist minister and a national retreat/conference/seminar speaker. He has spoken to over 400 churches, civic organizations, etc in 38 states in the U.S, and also Europe.

Roy is a published author and journalist who has written a book called "Caring for the Caregiver" written to help and encourage caregivers. He is an inspiraton writer for Wilson Living Magazine.

Roy recently launched a new national seminar titled "Living Beyond Grief". His website is www.royharris.info.

CRITICISM – Who Needs It?
By
Roy W. Harris
(roy@royharris.info)

Criticism is part of life. It may come from those who love us most or those who may not even like us. It may arrive like cold water poured on the flames of a great success or like stinging salt in the open wound of a setback. Have you ever seen a name pop up on your Caller ID and think; "oh no, what is it this time?" It almost seems that some people have the *gift* of criticism and feel they should *exercise* it at every opportunity.

Regardless of whether it is justified or not, receiving criticism is not normally a pleasant experience. How should we respond when we are criticized? Criticism offered with the right attitude and done in the right way can be a good thing. Criticism, when done in a constructive way to help us, may actually suggest ways to save us problems and create better situations for us.

While serving in my first pastorate, our church was growing and we desperately needed more room. Our church had a pre-school and we were in the process of expanding into a full blown Christian School. We formed the appropriate committees and made plans to construct a new educational building and cafeteria/fellowship hall. One committee member failed to attend any planning sessions and showed up at the final session shortly before the plans were to be presented to the church. After he'd looked over the plans, I asked him; "how do you like the plans?" He responded; "I don't." My young pastoral fervor got the best of me and I snapped back; "what don't you like about them?" It upset me that he failed to attend a single planning session and now he wanted to criticize the committee's work. He then showed me a major flaw in the plans. The restrooms were where the offices needed to be and vise/versa. He was absolutely right. We changed the plans and built the new building. I learned a valuable lesson from that experience about the value of criticism.

In Exodus chapter eighteen Moses' father-in-law Jethro brings Moses' wife and two sons to join him on his journey to the promise land. After a great time of celebration, Jethro observes Moses handling his daily leadership responsibilities. He correctly discerns that Moses is trying to do too much and will burn out quickly if something doesn't change. He truly has Moses and the children of Israel's welfare at heart.

Jethro first offers the criticism in verse 14 (Roy's paraphrase) Moses' father in law saw all that he was trying to do and ask if he realized what he was doing to these people. He goes on to tell Moses in verse 17 that what he was trying to do was not good. He then offers Moses a suggestion to help make the situation better. In verse 21 he encourages Moses to choose good qualified men to handle the small matters and save himself for the major issues that faced the people. Moses response provides us with a great step-by-step way of handling criticism.

Below are *four simple steps* that may be helpful as

you are confronted with criticism.

Step 1 - LISTEN to it. Moses heard Jethro out. Have you been introduced to someone you didn't know and became so busy thinking about what you should say and shaking the person's hand that you totally missed the person's name? A similar thing can  happen when we hear criticism. We sometimes throw up barriers because of who is delivering the criticism or simply because we are being criticized. We need to hold our tongues and *listen* to the details of the criticism before we *speak.* This does two things: 1. It helps us gain a better understanding of what we are dealing with and 2. It provides an opportunity for others to be heard. Even if we choose not to respond in the way others feel we should, they will feel that they've had a hearing. Many times just letting folks get it off their chests is all that is needed.

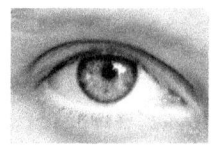 **Step 2 - LOOK** at it. Moses looked at the details of the plan Jethro had suggested. Once you've heard the criticism, thank the person for bringing it to your attention and tell them that you will certainly give it some thought. Then seriously examine the criticism/suggestion. Look at the merits of the criticism. Is this a valid criticism? Is there a problem that should be addressed? Are there changes that should be made? Is this person's suggestion the right way to go? You will then know if you should accept or reject the criticism.

Step 3 - LEARN from it. Moses recognized that Jethro was

right and implemented his suggestions. If you determine the criticism to be a valid one and the suggestions for change good ones, then don't let your pride hinder you from doing what your *gut* tells you that you should. Make the changes. Move in another direction. Implement a new procedure. Stop this or start that. We never reach the place that we cannot learn from others.

Step 4 - LIVE above it. After you've *LISTENED* to it, *LOOKED* at it, *LEARNED* from it and the criticism is unjust or not valid, what should you do? Choose to simply to *LIVE* above it. Sometimes the best response is not to respond at all. Do not spend a great deal of time rehashing the matter. Move on with life. File the criticism in the back of your mental filing cabinet and leave it there. Take the *high road* and continue doing what you're doing.

CRITICISM **– Who Needs It**? Criticism is part of life. It will come in times of great success and also great disappointment. It can be valid but it can also be bogus. It can be helpful and also hurtful. However it may come, we should do our best to handle it well.

What is your boss really thinking?

Dr. Roy W. Harris

Please come by my office, I need to talk with you a minute, you hear the boss say. Immediately your mind begins to take inventory of possible reasons for the meeting that will soon take place. You've met with the boss on numerous occasions for a variety of reasons. What could it be this time?

Have you wondered what the boss might be thinking when he or she; conducts an interview, gives assignments, doesn't give feedback, rants, or changes company policy? Well, from the point of view of someone who has been a boss for many years, I'll share some simple clues below that may help you better understand your boss and also help your boss to better understand you.

✓ The first thing to remember, *the boss is always the boss.* The boss knows this and you should always remember it. Don't back yourself into a corner because of pride and force the boss to act like the boss. Respect the position even if you have less respect for the person than the position.

✓ Another important thing to remember is *how you approach the boss* may directly impact *the way he approaches you.* If your *tone* or *body language* is *sarcastic* or *defensive,* the boss may immediately place himself *on the defensive.* A small matter may become bigger than it should.

✓ Try to remember *not* to take everything the boss says *personally.* A laugh or comment by the boss may only be an indication of a need for more information on the boss's part. Most of us make one major mistake over and over again. We think everything that the boss says or does is about us. It probably has more to do with needing additional information and less to do with us.

✓ Let the boss *guide the conversation*. You may get a clearer picture of what the boss is thinking by listening to what he or she says. Pay close attention to the words and not what you are going to say when you get an opening. Be careful about interrupting the boss. He may become irritated, perceiving your interruption as lack of respect or even rudeness.

✓ Find out what the boss is thinking by *asking questions*. Bosses usually do not mind and actually like good appropriate questions that will enable them better clarify their expectations and wishes. Questions like: *Were you thinking something different*? *What would you suggest*? *How might I approach this*? *Could you give a little more detail about what you are thinking*? Etc.

✓ Be *observant* of the *boss's demeanor*. Does he seem agitated or nervous? This could be an indication that he may have only a few minutes to talk with you or he has a pressing appointment or deadline. It may be better to excuse yourself and return later.

✓ Remember most bosses *don't like surprises* especially when they contain bad news. Bosses will not only be upset with the bad news, but they will also be upset when they don't receive a heads up before hand. The ranting and upset tone from the boss may point more to the fact he was not informed rather than because of the issue at hand.

✓ *Stop, breath, think* before you speak. Let the bosses words settle in your mind before you speak. Try not to react and speak to quickly. The emotion of the moment may cause you to misread what the boss means and you may say something that takes the conversation in a direction the boss did not intend. Choose words that that will respect the boss and provide opportunities to build a stronger relationship.

What is the boss really thinking? *Proverbs 25:6-7* provides good advice for learning what the boss might be thinking. Those verses encourage us to not exalt or promote ourselves in the front of the boss. But rather to wait for the boss to call us forward and to let us know what he or she's thinking.

You may not always know what the boss is thinking, but there are certainly good clues that may give you a good idea.

Spotlight On... Common Sense Leadership

As many know, Roy has been a WLM contributor for several years as well as our good friend. We are proud of his new writing endeavour and hope you all will pick up his latest book soon.

Roy's advice is immeasurable in these busy times that we lead.

BY ANGEL KANE

Q: What inspired you to write your latest book, Common Sense Leadership?

I began my first role in leadership at age 17, leading a crew of eight in a fast food restaurant. From then until now I've had the privilege of leading a variety of business, educational and religious organizations. Throughout the years I mentored many who worked under me. I wrote an article a few months back showcasing several common sense principles of leadership that I had employed and taught to others. After reading the article, several of those I had mentored encouraged me to expand the article into a practical book that could be used as a resource to help leaders at every level. I saw the need for a book.

Q: What are the characteristics of a good leader?

Wow, many books have been written on just such a topic. Integrity - be honest and forthright in all dealings. Balance - Good leaders lead like someone holding a bird, firm enough to keep control and loose enough to allow the organization to grow and develop without smothering it. Good people skills - a good leader must be able to relate to those he leads. The ability to communicate well is a must also. Good communication is essential to good mo-

Q: How does a leader go about inspiring those he works with?

There are a few important things a leader must remember if he wishes to maintain loyalty and inspire others to follow his leadership. First of all he must lead by example. He must show those he leads that he is willing to do the hard work and endure the same hardships and make the same sacrifices he expects of others. Others will be willing to go the extra mile if they believe he is willing to also.

Another important thing he should remember is to generously give credit for success to those he leads and accept blame with the team for problems or failures. The leader who remembers this will convey to those he leads that he values them highly and their work is appreciated.

A final important thing the leader should do is to genuinely care about the people he leads. People must feel their leader cares about them personally. Building strong relationships between the leader and those being led is something every leader must possess if he hopes to inspire others to follow his leadership.

Q: What's the best way to handle criticism from leaders, bosses or those whose we encounter in

Criticism will come if you do most anything or if you do nothing. It may come when you do well and or when you do poorly. But mark it down criticism will come. There are 4 things to remember when you are criticized.

First of all LISTEN TO IT. Hear the person out. Sometimes all they need to do is get it off their chest.

Secondly, LOOK AT IT. Ask yourself if the criticism in valued? Is it accurate?

Thirdly, if the criticism is a valid one, LEARN FROM IT. Make whatever adjustments or changes which may be needed.

Fourthly, what if the criticism is not valid? You've listened to it, looked at it and the criticism is not a just or valid one. If that's the case, simple learn to LIVE ABOVE IT. Just keep on doing what you are doing and do not let the criticism slow you down.

Q: What's the one thing you should never do as a leader?

There are a number of things that might qualify here, but one thing probably trumps them all. A wise leader must always thinks before he speaks. Reacting to personal emotions, the heat of the moment or apparent circumstances may cause a leader to say something or make a wrong decision that a few minutes and a little more information might have prevented.

Also, one should be careful about making

COMMON SENSE LEADERSHIP - Q & A

Roy W. Harris & Angel Kane

Q: What inspired you to write your latest book, Common Sense Leadership?

I began my first role in leadership at age 17 leading crew of eight in a fast food restaurant. From then until now I've had the privilege of leading a variety of business, educational and religious organizations. Throughout the years I mentored many who worked under me. I wrote an article a few months back showcasing several common sense principles of leadership that I had employed and taught to others. After reading the article, several of those I had mentored encouraged me to expand the article into a practical book that could be used as a resource to help leaders at every level. I saw the need for a book

Q: Who are the most influential leaders that you've encountered? What makes them stand out?

Q: What are the characteristics of a good leader?

Wow, many books have been written on just such a topic. Integrity – be honest and forthright in all dealings. Balance - Good leaders lead like someone holding a bird; firm enough to keep control and loose enough to allow the organization to grow and develop without smothering it. Good people skills – a good leader must be able to relate to those he leads. The ability to communicate well is a must also. Good communication is essential to good moral. Good leaders must have the ability to multi-task.

Q: How does a leader go about inspiring those he works with?

There are a few important things a leader must remember if he wishes to maintain loyalty and inspire others to follow his leadership. First of all he must lead by example. He must show those he leads that he is willing to do the hard work and endure the same hardships and make the same sacrifices he expects of others. Others will be willing to go the extra mile if they believe he is willing to also.

Another important thing he should remember is to generously give credit for success to those he leads and accept blame with the team for problems or failures. The leader who remembers this will convey to those he leads that he values them highly and their work is appreciated.

A final important thing the leader should do is to genuinely care about the people he leads. People must feel their leader cares about them personally. Building strong relationships between the leader and those being led is something every leader must possess if he hopes to inspire others to follow his leadership.

Q: What's the best way to handle criticism from leaders, bosses or those whose we encounter in our day-to-day life?

Criticism will come if you do most anything or if you do nothing. It may come when you do well and or when you do poorly. But mark it down criticism will come. There are 4 things to remember when you are criticized.

First of all LISTEN TO IT. Hear the person out. Sometimes all they need to do is get if off their chest.

Secondly, LOOK AT IT. Ask yourself if the criticism in valued? Is it accurate?

Thirdly, if the criticism is a valid one, LEARN FROM IT. Make whatever adjustments or changes may be needed.

Fourthly, what if the criticism is not valid? You've listen to it, looked at and the criticism is not a just or valid one. If that's the case, simple learn to LIVE ABOVE IT. Just keep on doing what you are doing and do not let the criticism slow you down.

Q: What's the one thing you should never do as a leader?

There are a number of things that might qualify here, but one thing probably trumps them all. A wise leader must always thinks before he speaks. Reacting to personal emotions, the heat of the moment or apparent circumstances may cause a leader to say something or make a wrong decision that a few minutes and a little more information might have prevented.

Also, one should be careful about making either of two absolute statements. One should never saw what he is *absolutely going to do* or what he *absolutely will never do*. Either one might of these statements make an unintended liar out of the leader at some point later on.

Q What tools can you tell us about that help us effectively use our time wisely in this busy world?

One of the best things to remember in using time wisely is to organize your priorities. There is a chapter in the book that discusses this in detail. The long and short of it is to organize your work three separate parts:
1. Things I must do at a certain time.   2. Things I must do but and no set time. 3. Things I would like to get if I have the time. Place items in your schedule moving from 1-3 in that order. You can plan your day, week, month and year using the above-mentioned formula. The book provides a detailed simple plan on how to do what you must get done and how to balance it with other things you'd like do.

Q: Roy, you stay very busy yourself, how to do find balance with your books, writing, speaking engagements, ministry and travel?

Balance is the key word. The most important thing is to plan your work and work your plan based on the solid foundation of your core priorities. Always keep *the main things, the main thing*.

My relationship with the LORD, comes first. I must maintain spiritual balance in order to maintain proper balance with my family and work responsibilities. My wife and family come next. The old expression *if mama isn't happy nobody's happy* rings very true. I know that if things are not as they should be at home that will impact everything I do outside my home. My wife (and my children right behind her) next to the LORD is the most important thing in my world. I love my work. I feel like I am the most fortunate and blessed man in the world.

Q: What new projects do you have in the works for 2014?

2014 looks to be another interesting year. I've been asked and am in the process of writing another book. My next book will probably be called <u>Commons Sense FAMILIES</u> or something similar. I began working with and helping families in my first pastorate many years ago and have continued that throughout the years. From that experience, I developed a 12 message sermon series on the family. The book comes from those sermons and will offer practical advice on; husband/relationships, what happens when the first child comes into the home, how to deal with a children two years old, teenagers in the house, financial planning for families and etc.

I'll be returning to Africa in the fall for the third time. I've been invited to speak in Uganda along with

Kenya, Rwanda and Burundi. I've begun and will continue working hard in 2014 to learn Swahili, the language of East Africa in an effort to better communicate with the African people.

A Diamond

By Roy Harris

A thought-provoking suggestion on how to fund future denominational outreach.

The story is told of a farmer in South Africa who sold his land and sought his fortune in diamonds. He found none and died penniless. After his death, gold was discovered on the very land that he had sold. He looked for treasure beyond his personal resources when more wealth than he could ever have imagined lay in a stream only a short distance from his farm house.

We must look deeply at our own resources as a denomination. God has blessed Free Will Baptists financially. By His hand we have made great strides since the formation of our National Association in 1935. Patterns and methods of support were established which have worked well.

Can we continue to operate using those same methods which have been in place for almost 70 years? How will we add to our missions outreach, expand our educational institutions and construct needed facilities on local, state and national levels?

Bold New Steps

While it is true that funding may be available from outside sources for some denominational enterprises, by and large, Free Will Baptists must pay their own way in fulfilling the role assigned by God to reach the world with the gospel. There is no golden formula that will solve all our denominational financial needs. We must become creative and future-thinking if we are to broaden our horizons and aggressively reach our world for Christ in the 21st century.

We must take bold new steps to face present and future needs which could not have been imagined by our denominational fathers.

Is there a resource available that could help propel our Free Will Baptist work to new levels in the 21st century? I believe there is. The Free Will Baptist Foundation is a vehicle our people can use to more effectively reach the world for Christ. The

A Diamond in the Rough
Roy W. Harris

The story is told of a farmer in South Africa who sold his land and sought his fortune in diamonds. He found none and died penniless. After his death, gold was discovered on the very land that he had sold. He looked for treasure beyond his personal resources when more wealth than he could ever have imagined lay in a stream only a short distance from his farmhouse.

We must look deeply at our own resources as a denomination. God has blessed Free Will Baptists financially. By His Hand we have made great strides since the formation of our National Association of Free Will Baptists in 1935. Patterns and methods of support were established which have worked well. Can we continue to operate using those same methods that have been in place for almost 70 years? How will we add to our missions out reach, expand our educational institutions and construct needed facilities on local state and national levels?

While it is true that funding may be available from out side sources for some denominational enterprises, by and large, Free Will Baptist must pay their own way in fulfilling the role assigned by God of reaching the world with the Gospel. There is no golden formula that will solve all our denominational financial needs. We must become creative and future thinking if we are to broaden our horizons and aggressively reach our world for Christ in the 21st century.

We must take bold new steps to face present and future needs, which could not have been imagined by our denominational fathers.

Is there a resource available that could help propel our Free Will Baptist work to new levels in the 21st century? I believe there is. Our Free Will Baptist Foundation is a vehicle that our people can use to more effectively reach the world for Christ. The Foundation is quickly approaching asset levels that will enable it to operate independently from the Board of Retirement and Insurance.

Due to staff limitations, the Free Will Baptist Foundation has been limited to primarily responding to requests by individuals and agencies for assistance with trust generation and funds management and disbursement. The department has done a commendable job with a limited amount of time and resources. Now is the time to begin thinking about the future role of the Foundation.

Stewardship responsibilities begin in the heart of every believer. We all hope to hear the Savior say some day: "well done thou good and faithful servant. Thou hast been faithful over a few things, I will make you ruler over many." Our goal should be to invest "where moth and rust doth not corrupt" and where the investment will pay eternal dividends. There is no substitute for personal responsibility and no doubt of personal accountability to God for the time, talent and treasure He has entrusted to each believer.

Stewardship training in our local churches is essential if believers are to truly understand individual responsibility and accountability. Pastors are the key to helping our people understand the Biblical mandate of stewardship. Other than the occasional sermon on tithing, pastors are sometimes at a loss on how to develop and implement a program of stewardship in our local churches. Most pastors would welcome help in this area. The Executive Office has developed materials on stewardship and made them available.

The ultimate aim of the Free Will Baptist Foundation should be helping believers manage their assets so they may be able to accomplish their personal stewardship goals. As the Foundation soon becomes of age, it can play a vital role in the development of a stewardship program for our denomination. The aim of this program would be to design, produce and distribute stewardship materials for our denomination. The program would help individuals, pastors, churches, local associations, state associations and national agencies develop stewardship plans and materials.

There is a desperate need for more help in our local churches in knowing how to determine readiness for new construction and how to design and implement capital campaigns for raising funds necessary for construction. This could be another arm of the stewardship role of the Foundation.

The Free Will Baptist Foundation can take on fresh look and a new name as it becomes independently recognized by our denomination. Maybe a name like the Free Will Baptist Foundation and Stewardship Department might be appropriate. (Realizing of course that a name change must be considered in light of present legal identity.)

This fresh old/new agency could serve as the flagship for the denomination in assisting our churches, local and national organizations and agencies in accumulating and managing funds for the purpose of extending the gospel at home and around the world.

The agency could serve our denomination by helping with stewardship in four areas:

- Assist individuals, churches, local & state associations/organizations and national agencies with advice, instruments for wills, trusts, etc. and management of funds received through these instruments.
- Assist individuals, pastors and churches with programs and stewardship materials for stewardship development on each level.
- Assist pastors, local churches, local & state associations/organizations with analysis and step-by-step procedures for investigating and launching capital campaigns.
- Assist pastors and local churches in discerning readiness for new construction.

The Free Will Baptist Foundation receives funds through the National Cooperative Plan of Support. It also receives management funds from revenue received made by the Foundation. Income for the department is nearing sufficient levels to adequately fund additional personnel. This department has the potential of becoming self-sufficient within a few years.

Free Will Baptists must take a hard look at how we hope to fund our work on all levels. The answer does not like in seeking resources from without. We possess the resources to fulfill the role God has assigned for Free Will Baptists.

Diamonds are rare and very valuable. Many times they are hidden and hard to find. The Free Will Baptist Foundation has been part of our denominational landscape for many years. We have yet to tap the potential of the Foundation. The Free Will Baptist Foundation is truly a diamond. It has great value and can play a vital role in the stewardship of the Free Will Baptist denomination. It may be a diamond in the rough now, but its glow will grow brighter with each passing year until Jesus returns.

The Interim Pastor

Dr. Roy W. Harris

The pastor informed the church of his decision to move to another ministry. He'll be leaving in 30 – 90 days. This is not the first time the church has begun the process of looking for a new pastor.

Who will shepherd the flock from now until the completed call of a new pastor? Pastor resignations often create a vacuum that will be filled by someone or group within the church. Each church decides its own approach to securing a new pastor but most churches scramble to find someone to fill the pulpit and lead the flock during the interim period.

Churches often look to retired ministers within their membership to fill the pulpit and provide spiritual nourishment. Churches may look outside their memberships for ministers in their communities who are willing step in for a few weeks until the church can complete its pastoral search. A deacon or layman may be pressed into service because there simply is no one else.

There is at least one other direction churches might look. They may select someone to serve as interim pastor until a new pastor can be secured.

Having the honor of serving four full-time churches and also as interim-pastor on four different occasions in other churches, I have a few suggestions to offer, which may aid local churches, district associations and state promotional directors in the development of a plan, profile, and financial package for the position of interim pastor.

Planning For Interim-Pastors

Free Will Baptist state promotional directors are confronted with the call from local churches with the need to help with the Pastoral search. They are often called upon to help fill pulpits while churches are traveling down the pastoral search road. This becomes even more difficult when multiple churches are without pastors at the same time.

State Promotional Directors in consultation with their executive committees, could select an appropriate number of ministers who would be willing to serve the churches in their states as interim pastors. They could begin with one man and add more as needed. This should not be an expense to the state. Local churches should be responsible for the financial compensation of interim pastors.

District associations could also take the initiative by formally designating a minister(s) within their association who would be willing to serve as interim pastors.

Having *go to men* who are eager to serve as interim pastors, would make it easier for our leaders and also provide a great resource to our churches.

Profile of Interim Pastors

Who are good choices to serve as Interim Pastors? Wisdom dictates that Interim Pastors have a minimum of five years pastoral experience and a proven track record. These men should be well known and well respected.

Life expectancy continues to rise. This offers a great opportunity for our Free Will Baptist Churches. Men who have given 30, 40 or even 50 years of service to our churches may be willing to give a little more. Retired ministers are a great resource and maybe one of the best choices to serve as Interim Pastors. Most ministers would agree that one may retire from pastoring, but one never retires from God's call to the ministry.

These Godly men are not interested or maybe able to take on the full gamut of the pastoral role, but are anxious to be used to help churches that need them. They have much to offer and churches can benefit greatly from their wealth of knowledge and experience.

Bi-vocational ministers who live in the general area of churches are another possible resource to fill the Interim Pastor's role.

Potential Interim Pastors should agree up front that they understand their role is not to become the pastor of the church, but to serve for a specific amount of time in the role of interim. This commitment should be made to the district or state association leaders and understood by all involved.

If a church approaches a minister who is serving as Interim Pastor with the possibility of him becoming their permanent pastor and he has an interest in becoming their pastor, then he must follow God's direction in the matter. But the Interim Pastor should not approach the church to suggest that he be considered as pastor.

The state and district associations may provide

a simple blueprint as a starting point for discussions between churches and potential interim pastors. This will help both parties to be on the same page as to the role, responsibilities, and expectations of both churches and interim pastors.

Interim pastors generally are not compensated at the same level as regular or full-time pastors. Therefore, churches should understand that interim pastors should not be expected to fulfill the responsibilities of a regular or full-time pastor.

A specific timeframe should be agreed upon at the outset by churches and ministers for the length of service for interim pastors. Three to six months is a good beginning point with an option to continue beyond the timeframe if agreed to by both parties. Churches who have recently gone through difficult or traumatic situations may want to consider a minimum of six months or longer with an interim pastor.

Many times churches expect interim pastors to step in and continue fulfilling all the responsibilities of their previous pastor. Wisdom dictates that churches and interim pastors have a clear understanding of what is expected of each. This understanding should be written down and agreed upon by both parties.

What should this agreement contain? Below is a brief outline of areas of responsibilities, which could serve as talking points between potential interim pastors and churches. It is a beginning point for the discussion. Each area should be discussed and agreed-upon.

Roles and Responsibilities For Churches & Interim Pastors

1. **Worship Responsibilities**
    a. The Interim will preach at each Sunday service or make sure pulpit is filled.
    b. Honorariums for substitute preachers will be the Interim Pastor's responsibility.
    c. The Church worship leader will plan the order of service.
    d. The Church will be responsible for selecting songs and arranging for special music.
    e. The Church will be responsible for preparing and printing the church bulletin. (Interim Pastor will communicate pertinent information).
    f. The Church will receive the offerings and take care of the announcements.

2. **Wednesday Prayer Meeting**
    a. The Interim Pastor will oversee prayer meetings, select, prepare and lead Bible studies and use others to lead at his discretion.

3. **Member Care** (Since Interim Pastors sometimes travel long distances to serve.)
    a. Much of personal member care will the done by phone.
    b. Interim Pastor will visit hospitals during member major surgeries and crisis times.
    c. Interim Pastor will not be required to be present for member outpatient procedures, tests, non-admittance Emergency Room illnesses, in-office

medical procedures, etc.
  d. Others will be responsible to step in case of death or other emergencies when the interim pastor is out of town or has prior responsibilities that make it impossible for him to be present.

4. Visitation
  a. The Interim Pastor will advise and provide counsel for the visitation program.
  b. Deacons and church leadership will be responsible for following up on first-time guests.

5. Boards & Committees
  a. The Interim Pastor work with and give direction to Church Leadership.
  b. He will meet with the Deacons as needed.
  c. He will meet with the Trustees as needed.
  d. He will meet with other groups, committees, boards and etc. as needed.
  e. He will work with and give direction to the Building Committee. (Work through and communicate with the chairman rather than all the committee members individually).

6. Interim Pastor's Wife's Involvement
  a. Her primary role is supporting the Interim Pastor.
  b. She is eager to serve, but cannot commit to specific responsibilities until she determines which areas she would like to serve in and will fit with her schedule and gifts.
  c. Her job responsibilities, work hours and

distance to the church may impact her ability to attend prayer meeting every week. The church must understand when she cannot be present.

7. Business Meetings
a. The Church and Interim Pastor should decide who would be responsible for moderating the church business meetings.

8. Final Considerations
a. Reminder – The Interim Pastor has responsibilities outside the church. He must be allowed to fulfill his obligations in addition to taking on the role of Interim Pastor.
b. The Interim Pastor will receive a weekly salary; *(amount agreed upon by pastor and church. Churches & Interim Pastors should keep in mind distance to and from the pastor's home to the church.)*
c. The church will supply Sunday lunch for the Interim Pastor and his family.
d. The church will make arrangements for a place for the Interim Pastor and his family to rest and study on Sunday afternoons between Sunday services.
e. The church parsonage could be made available for the Interim Pastor's use on weekends. This could be a great benefit to the church. The Interim Pastor might be able to arrive on Saturdays and leave on Mondays instead of driving back and forth long distances on Sundays.

Interim Pastors fill a vital role in the lives of our

churches. Churches may be without pastors for extended periods of time. The Interim Pastor can step in, supply spiritual nourishment, and serve as a leader to help our churches the interim period.

District and state leaders could serve as great facilitators in designating men of their choosing who are willing to serve as Interim Pastors and connect them with local churches. They may also provide suggested talking points necessary for an agreement that would place potential Interim Pastors and churches on the same page.

Who comes to your mind that would make a great Interim Pastor? We have great men who still have a lot to give. Let's make use of this tremendous virtually untapped resource.

It's Just
GOOD BUSINESS

BY ROY HARRIS

For some, the very mention of the term *business meeting* sends a shiver up the spine, much like being reminded of an upcoming root canal. Business meetings create dread, anxiety, sometimes even fear, especially when difficult issues must be addressed. Yet business meetings, whether at the local church, district, state, or national level are necessary in the Free Will Baptist autonomous form of church government.

While you may never experience a sense of euphoria about an upcoming business meeting, you can defeat the dread and make meetings run more smoothly and successfully by considering the following suggestions:

Be punctual. Start the meeting on time. This sets the tone for the meeting and demonstrates respect for those in attendance.

Be prepared. Advance preparation helps the meeting stay focused and saves time. Good preparation includes an agenda, listing each item to be addressed. (Consider the sample agenda on the next page.)

Be productive. The following helpful hints—common sense, really—will help you get the most from your meeting.

- Ask that all discussion, comments, and questions be directed to the moderator. (This will help keep order and keep differences of opinion from getting out of hand.)
- Always get a motion and second on the floor before allowing discussion. This will help keep the discussion from wandering and wasting time.
- A motion is not a motion until the moderator recognizes it, repeats it, and asks for a second.
- After a motion and second, allow ample time for discussion, but don't allow the debate to drag on indefinitely.

Know Your Motions. Three types of motions generally arise in business meetings: main motions, incidental motions, and motions to bring a question back to the assembly. The list below cites common motions that arise in business meetings.

Main Motions (Ordered by priority. Any motion below can be made, and is in order, if it appears higher on the list than the one already made below it.)

- *Motion to adjourn:* Everyone enjoys this motion as it signals an end to the meeting. However, the motion to adjourn cannot interrupt a person speaking, requires a second, is not debatable, cannot be amended, and requires a majority vote.
- *Motion to table* (or lay on the table): Defers an item of business to another time. It must meet the following requirements: It cannot interrupt a person speaking, requires a second, is not debatable, cannot be amended, and requires a majority vote. *Note:* Outside the United States, to table a motion means you make the item available for consideration.
- *Motion for previous question:* Calls for an end to discussion. It cannot interrupt a person speaking, requires a second, is not debatable, cannot be amended, and requires a two-thirds majority.
- *Motion to postpone:* Delays the action as determined by the body. It cannot interrupt a person speaking, requires a second, is not debatable, cannot be amended, and requires a majority vote.
- *Motion to refer the matter to a committee:* Defers the item of business to a smaller subsection of the voting body. A committee is often used when more research is required or details need to be handled outside of a public forum. It cannot interrupt a person speaking, requires a second, is not debatable, cannot be amended, and requires a majority vote.
- *Motion to amend:* Adds to or alters an existing motion to make it more acceptable to the voting body, usually based on discussion. It cannot interrupt a person speaking, requires a second, is not debatable, cannot be amended, and requires a majority vote.
- *Motion to postpone indefinitely:* This motion effectively kills the item of business. It cannot interrupt a person speaking, requires a second, is not debatable, cannot be amended, and requires a majority vote.

It's Just Good Business
Dr. Roy W. Harris

The mere mention of the words *business meeting* can sometimes send a shiver up the spine generating the anticipation similar to that of an upcoming root canal. Business meetings are absolutely essential to the operation of many organizations. Whether high school groups, college faculty or student organizations, neighborhood associations or watch groups, local churches and their auxiliaries, government governing bodies such city councils, state legislatures and their various appointed or elected committees, corporate board rooms or stockholder meetings, and many others all have prescribed formats for approving previous actions, planning new endeavors and authorizing income collection and expenditures for the organizations.

The local church or district, state and national associations are necessary in our Free Will Baptist autonomous form of church government. Many times they are approached with dread, anxiety and sometimes fear. Although feelings of euphoria may never be experienced when reminded of an upcoming business meeting, there are ways to make it run more smoothly ending in a successful outcome. Here are a few things that might help your business meeting run more smoothly.

Be punctual – Begin the meeting on time. Starting on time sets a tone of readiness and shows respect for the time of those in attendance.

Be prepared – Good preparation will help the meeting to *stay on track* and also keep it focused. Keeping focused will save time. Good preparation should include the use of an *Agenda of business* for the meeting listing each item, which should be addressed. Below is a sample:

MEETING AGENDA
    i. Call the meeting to order.
    ii. Recognize and seat the delegates (have them stand).
        1. Standing Delegates
            a. Church members for local church meetings.
            b. Ordained ministers and deacons for local, state and national association meetings.
        2. Elected Delegates
            a. From local churches for district meetings.
            b. From district meetings for state associations.
        3. Announce that this will be the voting body for this session and have them be seated.
    iii. Recognize the Clerk/Secretary for the written record of the previous meeting's proceedings (minutes).
        1. If these are printed and have been distributed, there may not be a need to read them

aloud. Again, this will save time.
2. Ask if there are any additions or corrections, if there are none, approve them as read (no motion needed – this will save time.)

iv. Recognize the Treasurer to give the financial report.
1. Ask for a motion to receive the report and for a second.
2. Ask for any questions or comments.
3. Take the vote. (It's usually best to vote when money or resources are mentioned.)

v. Board & Committee reports (follow same procedure as iv.)
1. It's always best to have the major board or committee report first. Advisory or Deacon board in local church business meetings and the Executive Committee/Board report on the district and state levels. Other board/committee reports should follow.
   a. This may be more appropriate immediately following the seating of the delegates if issues to be covered warrant it.

vi. Review any unfinished business from previous meetings (Old business).
vii. Ask if there is any new business to come before the body.
viii. When you've covered your last item, ask for a motion to adjourn.

Be productive
- Helpful Hints
    i. Ask that all discussion, comments and questions be directed to the moderator. (This will help keep order and keep differences of opinion between individuals from getting out of hand.)
    ii. Always get a motion and a second on the floor before beginning the discussion. This will help keep the discussion from wandering, chasing rabbits and wasting time.
    iii. A motion is not a motion until you recognize it, repeat it and ask for a second.
    iv. After the motion and second allow ample time for discussion but don't allow it to drag on indefinitely. An easy approach is to look from one side of the room to the other and if you do not see or hear from anyone, say something like "hearing none, all in favor of the motion please say aye." Take the vote and move on.

- Know Your Motions (You may want to keep a copy of the motions listed below with you as a reference when moderating business meetings.)
    i. There are three types of motion that generally arise in business meetings; *Main Motions, Incidental Motions* and *Motions that bring a question again back to the assembly*. Below is a list of motions that commonly arise in business meetings.
    ii. *Main Motions* (Listed in order of priority. A motion below can be made and is in order if it is higher on the list than one already made below it.)
        1. *Motion to Adjourn* – Cannot interrupt a person speaking, needs a 2nd, not debatable, cannot be amended and requires only a majority vote.
        2. *Motion to Lay on the Table* – Cannot interrupt the person speaking, needs a 2nd, not debatable, cannot be amended and requires only a majority vote.
        3. *Motion for The Previous Question* – Cannot interrupt the person speaking, needs a 2nd, not debatable, cannot be

amended and requires a 2/3rd vote.
4. *Motion to Postpone the matter to a later time* – Cannot interrupt the person speaking, needs a 2nd, is debatable, can be amended and requires only a majority vote.
5. *Motion to Refer the matter to a Committee* – Cannot interrupt the person speaking, needs a 2nd, is debatable, can be amended and requires only a majority vote.
6. *Motion to Amend the Motion* (this may be done by adding a word or phrase, by deleting words or by offering an entirely different motion) – Cannot interrupt a person speaking, needs a 2nd, is debatable, can be amended once and requires only a majority vote.
7. *Motion to Postpone Indefinitely* (this kills the motion) – Cannot interrupt someone who is speaking, requires a 2nd, is debatable, cannot be amended and requires only a majority vote.

iii. *Incidental Motions* (No order of

priority and are dealt with immediately)
1. *Point of Order* – Can interrupt someone speaking, does not require a 2nd, not debatable, cannot be amended and no vote is taken, moderator decides the validity of the point made.
2. *Appeal the Decision of the Chair* (when an individual does not agree with the moderators ruling) – Can interrupt someone speaking, requires a 2nd, is debatable, cannot be amended and requires only a majority vote.
3. *Motion to Suspend the Rules* (in affect permits the body's action to supersede the established rules) – Cannot interrupt someone speaking, requires a 2nd, not debatable, cannot be amended and requires a $2/3^{rd}$ vote.
4. *Object to the consideration of the motion* – Can interrupt a person speaking, does not need a 2nd, not debatable, cannot be amended and requires a $2/3^{rd}$ vote.

iv. *Motions that bring a previous motion*

back to the assembly.
1. *Remove from the Table* (brings back for consideration an earlier motion which had been tabled) – Cannot interrupt a person speaking, requires a 2nd, not debatable, cannot be amended and requires only a majority vote.
2. *Rescind a Previous Motion* (reverse an action already agreed on) – Cannot interrupt a person speaking, must be made by a person who voted for the previously adopted motion, requires a 2nd, is debatable, can be amended and requires a majority vote providing the body has been notified ahead of time.

Business meetings can help churches and associations accomplish their missions and set a course for future success. Following the suggestions given earlier will not guarantee success, but they should make your business meetings more productive and run more smoothly. They might just relieve a little stress, anxiety and maybe even fear and save you the cost of some Rolaids or Maalox.

What's It Worth?

By Roy W. Harris

How do you determine the value of anything? That can be both an easy and hard question to answer. I recently read a study on the value of the materials, which compose the human body, published by Imperial State Institute for Nutrition at Tokyo. Their study concluded that the most valuable part of the human body is our skin. According to the study, skin is worth 25 cents per square foot, and the average person's skin is worth about $3.50. (How they arrive at that value, and why anyone would even want to know is anybody's guess.) The U.S. Bureau of Chemistry and Soils lists the other chemicals and minerals contained in our bodies as 65% Oxygen, 18% Carbon, 10% Hydrogen, 3% Nitrogen, 1.5% Calcium, 1% Phosphorous, 0.35% Potassium, 0.25% Sulfur, 0.15% Sodium, 0.15% Chlorine, 0.05% Magnesium, 0.0004% Iron, 0.00004% Iodine with traces of fluorine, silicon, manganese, zinc, copper, aluminum, and arsenic. Pretty impressive list, huh? Well, according to U.S. Bureau of Chemistry and Soils, the value of those chemicals comes to one dollar. So the value our skin and the other materials that make up the human body, come to a grand total of $4.50. We'll come back to that in a few minutes.

It's easy to determine value when you have a standard to measure value with like the "Blue Book" for cars, trucks and motorcycles, the daily per ounce price of gold or per dollar price of a gallon of gasoline. But other things are not so easily calculated. How do place value on the feeling you experience when holding your newborn child or grandchild for the first time, or seeing your soon-to-be-bride walking down the aisle, or your soon-to-be-husband waiting at the alter. Some things just cannot be measured in dollars and cents. They go much deeper. It is nice to possess things, and things bring a measure of happiness, but the reality is that things wear out, become boring or obsolete and the temporary happiness they bring is fleeting.

True contentment comes with things that cannot be measured by any tangible standard. Friends, family, personal contentment and peace with God all play important roles in who we are. How do you measure the worth of these important things?

It's been said that if a person has three close lifelong friends who can be trusted and counted on then he or she is a rich person. True friends love you for who you are and not for what you possess. Many times they are closer than family members and may be sought out for advice, counsel or just a listening ear to hear our dreams, frustrations and hurts. Take it from Solomon, one of the wisest men who ever lived: *A man that hath friends must show himself friendly and there is a friend that sticketh closer than a brother.* Good friends are a special gift – their value is far beyond measure.

'Blood is thicker than water' - we've all heard that expression. It has also been said that most of us are the sum total of all those who've invested their lives into ours. We owe much to family. They gave us life itself. At birth, they helped us when we were helpless. They provided food, shelter and clothing to sustain us. They protected us from dangers that surrounded us. They were the first in line in teaching us the basics of life. No matter what happens, most of us can count on family. How much is that worth? The value of family is immeasurable. We are truly wealthy if we are blessed with great families.

Some people spend their entire lives trying to find Personal Contentment. Many times contentment is sought after in all the wrong places. We assess our value as persons based on wrong standards of measurement. The way to Personal Contentment is not found in the size of our bank accounts, the type of cars we drive, the degrees we've earned, the careers we've chosen or accomplishments we've achieved. All of those and other things bring a sense of satisfaction and rightly

What's It Worth?

By Roy W. Harris

How do you determine the value of anything? That can be both an easy and hard question to answer. I recently read a study on the value of the materials that compose the human body by Imperial State Institute for Nutrition at Tokyo. Their study concluded that the most valuable part of the human body is our skin. According to the study, skin is worth 25 cents per square foot and the average person's skin is worth about $3.50. (How they arrive at that value and why anyone would even want to know is anybody's guess.)

The U.S. Bureau of Chemistry and Soils list the other chemicals and minerals contained in our bodies as 65% Oxygen, 18% Carbon, 10% Hydrogen, 3% Nitrogen, 1.5% Calcium, 1% Phosphorous, 0.35% Potassium, 0.25% Sulfur, 0.15% Sodium, 0.15% Chlorine, 0.05% Magnesium, 0.0004% Iron,

0.00004% Iodine with traces of fluorine, silicon, manganese, zinc, copper, aluminum, and arsenic. Pretty impressive list huh? Well, according to U.S. B of C & Soils the value of those chemicals comes to a dollar. So the value our skin and the other materials that make up the human body come to a grand total of $4.50. We'll come back to that in a few minutes.

It's easy to determine value when you have a standard to measure value with like the *"Blue Book"* for cars, trucks and motorcycles, the daily per ounce price of gold or per dollar price of a gallon of gasoline. But other things are not so easily calculated. How do place value on the feeling you experience when holding your new born child or grandchild for the first time , or seeing your soon to be bride walking down the aisle, or your soon to be husband waiting at the alter. Some things just cannot be measured in dollars and cents. They go much deeper. It is nice to possess *things* and things bring a measure of happiness, but the reality is that things wear out, become boring or obsolete and the temporary happiness they bring is fleeting.

True contentment comes with things, which cannot be measured by any tangible standard. Friends, Family, Personal Contentment and Peace with God all play important roles in who we are. How do you measure the worth of these important things?

It's been said that if a person has three close lifelong friends who can be trusted and counted on he or she is a rich person. True friends love you for who you are and not for what you possess. Many times they are closer than family members and may be sought out for advice, council or just a *listening ear* to hear our dreams, frustrations and hurts. Take it from Solomon, one of the wisest men who ever lived; A man that hath friends must show himself friendly and *there is a friend that sticketh closer than a brother*. Good friends are a special gift – their value is far beyond measure.

Blood is thicker than water, we've all heard that expression. It has also been said that most of us are the *sum total* of all those who've invested their lives into ours. We owe much to family. They gave us life itself. At birth, they helped us when we were helpless. They provide food, shelter and clothing to sustain us. They protect us from dangers that surrounded us. They were the first in line in teaching us the basics of life. No matter what happens, most of us can count on family. How much is that worth? The value of family is immeasurable. We are truly wealthy if we are blessed with great families.

Some people spend their entire lives trying to find *Personal Contentment*. Many times contentment is sought after in all the wrong places. We assess our value as persons based on wrong standards of measurement. The way to *Personal Contentment* is not found in the size of our bank accounts, the type cars we drive, the degrees we've earned, the careers we've chosen or accomplishments we've achieved. All of those and other things bring a sense of satisfaction and rightly so. We work hard and our hard work is rewarded.

Personal Contentment is more valuable than anything we can accomplish or own. It is much deeper. *Personal Contentment* is found in personal worth. It is *what we are* and not what we possess, what we *accomplish* or what *others think* of us. Our personal worth is how we see ourselves deep down inside. In order to be contented, we must be satisfied with who we are. We are all uniquely created in God's image. Not a single one of us have identical fingerprints or DNA. We are not too small or too tall. We are all *special* in God's eyes. We need to become *ok* in our own skins. If we are not, then we should ask ourselves what is necessary to become *ok*? If changes in personal behavior, our treatment of others and etc. become apparent in our own minds, then we must do what is necessary to become pleased with who we are. Many times we need God's help in making some of those changes.

What's it worth is a question asked many times about many things. The pure material value of the human body is about $4.50. The worth of human being is beyond measure. You can always acquire more *things* but more *things* will only bring temporary satisfaction. Want to find *Personal Contentment*? Remember it's not what you own but *whom you are* deep down inside that makes the difference. The U.S. Army has a saying: "Be all you can be." I have another one: "Be content with who you are" and deep down inside and you'll "find the *Personal Contentment* in life you're looking for."

What's *Personal Contentment* worth? It's priceless but it is also free to everyone.

Thank You Very Much

By ROY W. HARRIS

While growing up I remember hearing a bluegrass mountain tune titled "Give Me The Flowers While I'm Living" with an interesting message.

One verse and refrain from the song said: *In this world is where we need our flowers, A kind word to help us get along, If you can't give me flowers while I'm living, Please don't send them when I'm gone. Won't you give me my flowers while I'm living, Let me enjoy them while I can, Please don't wait till I'm ready to be buried, And then slip some flowers in my hand.*

The song emphasized how important it is for people to know they've made a difference in the lives of others. The message of the song is to let others know while they are still with us rather than wishing we had said something after death takes them on and it's too late.

Proverbs 3:27 in the Bible tells us that we should not *withhold good from those who deserve it, when we have the power to show good to them.* This is a simple principle with a broad application. In the framework of this article it could be said like this: *if there are some deserving people who've impacted your life, there is a way you can let them know, it's your duty to tell them.*

After receiving news that a dear man who'd been my teacher, mentor, colleague and friend had passed away, I began to think not only of him but many others who'd impacted me and helped mold and shape my life. I realized that even though they'd contributed much to building the total person I am today and I appreciated all they'd done to stretch and build me as a person, I'd never let them know what a tremendous impact they'd made on my life. This caused me to begin thinking about the importance of Proverbs 3:27 and how I should do something about it. A number of people immediately came to mind. I began a list of those people and titled it, "People who have influenced my life." I jotted down specific things I'd learned from those people and how each one had impacted me. My goal was to try and think of at least 10 people. Later in this article I'll list the 10 and some specific ways they made a difference in my life.

I would encourage you to consider doing something similar. Here's a simple plan on how to you can say *thank you* to those special people. (1) Spend time thinking about special people who've impacted your life and make a list of those people. (2) Beside each person's name, jot down one or two things you learned and how they impacted your life (and may still

be). (3) Determine those who may possibly be contacted. (4) Develop a plan for contacting each one (email, card, letter, phone call, etc.) (5) Contact these people one at a time to say *thank you* while keeping your list of how each one impacted you handy. (6) Jot down notes of those you are able to reach and how they responded to you. (7) When you finish, take a minute to thank the good Lord for all those special people.

You've had time to think about some of those *special people* who've made profound contributions to who you are as a person. Now it's your turn. The old Biblical expression *do unto others* still remains true today but let's turn it around a little. *Others have already done unto (invested in) you,* now it's your turn to invest in the lives of others. Every day in small or large ways you impact the lives of others. Keep in mind people are listening and watching what you say and do and how you react to life's frustrations, disappointments, triumphs and failures. You've probably already influenced people in ways yet to be realized by you. Who knows, maybe one

---

"People who have in[fluenced my life]"

Mom – Take pride in how you dress, if you work hard you can achieve much in life.

Dad – Be faithful to your God, your family and your church. Get up every day and go to work. Anything worth doing is worth doing right.

My Grandparents – Made me feel special and about the most important person in the world (I'm trying to pass that feeling on to my five grandchildren as well.)

Mr. Leonard (5-6 elementary basketball and track coach and teacher) – Taught me to love sports and to play by the rules.

Big John – (My first regular job boss) – Trusted me with a restaurant night manager position at age 17 and helped me believe I could take on most anything and be successful.

Mrs. Laura Thaggen (College Freshman Speech Teacher) – Taught me to stand tall and speak up in front of others.

Dr. Charles Thaggen (My College President and later my boss) – Exampled for me how to be loyal to those who work under you and stand with them even when you may not always agree with every decision they make. Also, always ask the important questions.

Dr. Stanley Outlaw (College Professor) – Taught me foundational biblical knowledge that has served as a bedrock upon which much has been built.

Mr. Ralph Hampton (College Professor) – Led me to memorize scripture that has both sustained and been a great resource for personal soul winning, sermon preparation and helping others through difficult days. He taught me the basics of how to look at a passage of scripture, understand its meaning, glean from it biblical principles and apply those principles to daily life, i.e., the basic parts of sermon and how to put a sermon together.

Miss Peggy Jo McElhiney – How important it is to serve quietly in the background never seeking recognition or reward a[nd]...

Thank You Very Much

By Roy W. Harris

While growing up I remember hearing a bluegrass mountain tune titled **_Give Me The Flowers While I'm Living_** with an interesting message. One verse and refrain from the song said: *In this world is where we need our flowers, A kind word to help us get along, If you can't give me flowers while I'm living, Please don't send them when I'm gone. Won't you give me my flowers while I'm living, Let me enjoy them while I can, Please don't wait till I'm ready to be buried, And then slip some flowers in my hand.*

The song emphasized how important it is for people to know they've made a difference in the lives of others. The message of the song is to let others know while they are still with us rather than wishing we had said something after death takes them on and it's too late.

Proverbs 3:27 in the bible tells us that we should not *withhold good from those who deserve it, when we have the power to show good to them.* This is a simple principle with a broad application. In the framework of this article it could be said like this; *if there are some deserving people who've impacted your life, and there is a way you can let them know, it's your duty to tell them.*

After receiving news that a dear man who'd been my teacher, mentor, colleague and friend had passed away, I began to think not only of him but many others who'd impacted me and helped mold and shape my life. I realized that even though they'd contributed much to building the total person I am today and I appreciated all they'd done to stretch and build me as a person, I'd never let them know what a tremendous impact they'd made on my life. This caused me to begin thinking about the importance of Proverbs 3:27 and how I should do something about it. A number of people immediately came to mind. I began a list of those people and titled it; *People who have influenced my life.* I jotted down specific things I'd learned from those people and how each one had impacted me. My goal was to try and think of at least 10 people. Later in this article I'll list the ten and some specific ways they made a difference in my life.

I would encourage you to consider doing something similar. Here's a simple plan on how to you can say *thank you* to those special people. (1) Spend time thinking about special people who've impacted your life and make a list of those people. (2) Beside each person's name, jot down one or two things you learned and how they impacted your life (and may still be). (3) Determine those who may possibly be contacted. (4) Develop a plan for contacting each one (email, card, letter, phone call, etc.). (5) Contact these people one at a time to say *thank you* while keeping your list of how each one impacted you handy. (6) Jot down notes of those you are able to reach and how they responded to you. (7) When you finish, take a minute to thank the good Lord for all those special people.

People who have influenced my life.

Mom – Take pride in how you dress. If you work hard you can achieve much in life.

Dad – Be faithful to your God, your family and your church. Get up every day and go to work. Anything worth doing is worth doing right. .

My Grandparents – Made me feel special and about the most important person in the world (I'm trying to pass that feeling on to my 5 grandchildren as well.)

Mr. Leonard (5-6 elementary basketball and track coach & teacher) - Taught me to love sports and to play by the rules.

Big John – (My first regular job boss) - Trusted me with a restaurant night manager position at age 17 and helped me believe I could take on most anything and be successful.

Mrs. Laura Thigpen (College Freshman Speech Teacher) – Taught me to stand tall and speak up in front of others.

Dr. Charles Thigpen(My College President and later my boss) – Exampled for me how to be loyal to those who work under you and stand with them even when you may not always agree with every decision they make. Also, always ask the important questions.

Dr. Stanley Outlaw (College Professor)– Taught me foundational biblical knowledge that has served as a bedrock upon which much has been built.

Mr. Ralph Hampton(College Professor) – Led me to memorize scripture that has both sustained and been a great resource for personal soul winning, sermon preparation and helping others through difficult days. He taught me the basics of how to look at a passage of scripture, understand its' meaning, glean from it biblical principles and apply those principles to daily life. IE – The basic parts of sermon and how to put a sermon together.

Miss Peggy Jo McElhiney – How important it is to serve quietly in the background never seeking recognition or reward and you can profoundly impact an organization.

Sparky – Never take anything that doesn't belong to you, it can get you into a lot of trouble; (He did both.)

Mr. Leroy Forlines – Helped me develop my beliefs in basic theology and how to find solid biblical answers to the most difficult questions in life.

Chaplain Billy Lord (my boss in the U.S. Army) – Learn to delegate. You'll accomplish a lot more with others helping you.

Mr. Glenn Thomas (my father-in-law)– Taught me the value of tapping into the wisdom of those who have more experience and who've gone down the path ahead of you.

Mr. Alton Raines (one of my deacons in Ahoskie, NC) – Taught me the value of listening to those who may disagree with you. They may just have a good point that should be looked at.

Mrs. Dorothy Early – Taught me how an older Christian Lady should carry herself and also devotion to a mate who can no longer care for himself.

Mr. Sheldon Lance (one of my deacons in Asheville, N.C.) – Don't be afraid of technology, embrace it.

Mr. Jim Horne – Sacrifice if necessary to do the right thing. Others will remember you long after you're gone. Also, love and appreciate your pastor.

Rev. Bob Shockey – Give to others. It will come back

to you many fold.

Rev. Mance Cason – Be faithful at what you do and don't use age as an excuse for sitting on the sidelines.

Amy Harris (my lovely wife) – How to love through adversity with class and dignity.

Diana Harris (my first wife who died from cancer) – Showed how to face a terminal disease and death with courage and trust in the Lord.

You've had time to think about some of those *special people* who've made profound contributions to who you are as a person. Now it's your turn. The old Biblical expression *do unto others* still remains true today but let's turn it around a little. *Others have already done unto (invested in) you* now it's your turn to invest in the lives of others. Every day in small or large ways you impact the lives of others. Keep in mind people are listening and watching what you say and do and how you react to life's daily frustrations, disappointments, triumphs and failures.

You've probably already influenced people in ways yet to be realized by you. Who knows, maybe one day someone will call or email you a hand full thank yous and you may find out what a difference your life truly is making. It's time to say *Thank You*. Go ahead, give some of those flowers out now. Don't just take my word or it. Remember that great Biblical Principle in Proverbs 3:27.

KEEPING IT TOGETHER

By ROY HARRIS

Have you ever found yourself torn between *family responsibilities* and *a job*?

Have you heard it said that if you want something done, give it to the busiest person in the room and then you seem to end up being that person?

Have you gotten a little irritable and maybe lost your patience or temper when others failed to act or perform the way you felt they should; only later realizing that you misread the situation or overreacted because of the stress you were under?

Unfortunately, this happens to some of the nicest people.

Personal needs, family life, and job responsibilities…how in the world can we *keep it all together*?

I've been in some form of management or leadership role, with all the pressures that go with it, most of my adult life. I'm certainly no expert and each person's situation is unique, but there are some basic principles which seem to help and hold true in most situations.

Priorities

If we are to keep IT together, then we should remember what IT is.

IT is our lives as a whole.

Our lives are made up of a combination of relationships and each one requires a certain amount of our time, talent and even treasure. How we manage these relationships directly impacts our health and happiness. I once heard a man make a redundant statement which really is true: "Always keep the *main thing* the *main thing*." Keeping the main thing the main thing requires a balancing act of sorts and requires making choices.

How do we make good choices? By deciding what is most important to us.

Our personal lives could be divided into two areas; our *private* and *public lives*. If we are going to keep it all together we must find a way to balance these two.

Private Life

Our private lives bring fulfillment and happiness which can never come from anywhere else.

This is a very important principle to remember.

Our private lives are made up of three key relationships; our relationship with ourselves, our family and our maker. Happiness and contentment begins with being at peace with one's self. Finding personal time on a regular basis to do something you enjoy must be done on purpose and usually doesn't happen by accident. Good emotional and physical health directly impacts our other relationships. Sacrificing for others is noble, but failing to attend to one's personal needs will eventually have a negative impact on both our private and public lives.

Our family relationships must trump our public lives. Unhappiness at home will translate into less effectiveness outside the home. Our families must know and believe that they are more important than anything in our public lives. They would much rather spend time with us than to have us spend money on them. Instead of talking about the things we bought for them as kids, my grown children mention far more often the times we took them fishing, bowling or to Chucky Cheese.

Public Life

Our public lives are made up of a number of key relationships also; our friends, our jobs, church family and others. More often than not, our public lives complicate our private lives.

If we make our private lives a priority then it will help us better manage our public lives.

If we are employed outside the home, there are certain demands which come with the job. We expect a certain amount of our time and talent to be devoted to the job. The Bible reminds us that we have a responsibility to take care of our family's needs. Adam actually had the first human job of *dressing & keeping* the Garden of Eden. So work is an honorable thing, but we must be careful not to allow work to become the dominant thing. Molding children and growing with a mate are far more important than making money.

We are created with a built-in need for social interaction with others. Friends, church family, community involvement are all important. They fulfill a need to be with people, contribute to society and make a difference in the lives of others.

Involvement with others outside the home, however, must be governed by what we realistically have time to do.

That is also another great principle to remember.

It's OK to say NO! No is sometimes the appropriate answer in some situations. One thing about it, you can never please all the people all the time so do what you feel in your heart is the best thing each time.

Practical Principles for *Keeping IT Together*

Planning for work and play should be focused through the lens of personal priorities.

Our personal peace and contentment directly impacts other relationships.

Private life commitments should be considered first and take priority over our public life.

Remember your children will be all grown up before you know it. Do *NOW* what you will wish you had done later.

The greatest thing you can do for your children is to love your spouse. Make time for and work hard on making that a high priority.

The Scriptures remind us that one's close relationship with our heavenly Father has a positive, direct impact on our personal peace and contentment.

The Bible has a great book called Proverbs written by a wise King named Solomon. It's one of the most practical works on keeping IT all together that I've read. The book has 31 chapters and provides practical principles for private and public relationships. A great suggestion is to read one chapter each day using the day of the month as a guide and reading an extra chapter or two on the last day of the month, with months which have less than 31 days. You might be surprised how much practical wisdom you'll find in just 31 short days.

Sometimes trying to *keep IT all together* seems impossible! However, if you do your best *to keep the main thing the main thing*, you will be amazed how the *other things* fall into place.

Keeping It Together

By
Dr. Roy W. Harris

Have you ever found yourself torn between *family responsibilities* and the *job*? Have you heard it said that if you want something done, give it to the busiest person in the room and then you seem to end up being that person? Have you had to make a choice between your child's *special* event, your spouse's *needs* or meeting a work related deadline? Have you said yes one too many times and overfilled your personal plate? Have you found yourself with two or more major projects or jobs that need to be completed and feeling the pressure of not knowing if you can finish them on time? Have you gotten a little irritable and maybe lost your patience and/or temper when others failed to act or perform the way you felt they should; only later realizing that you misread the situation or overreacted because of the stress you were under? Unfortunately, this happens to some of the nicest people.

Personal needs, family life, and job responsibilities….How in the world can *we keep it all together?* I've been in some form of management or leadership role, with all the pressures that go with it, most of my adult life. I am certainly no expert and each person's situation is unique but there are some basic principles, which seem to help and hold true in most situations.

Priorities

If we are to keep *IT...* together then we should remember what *IT...* is. *IT....* is our lives as a whole. Our lives are made up of a combination of relationships and each one requires a certain amount of our time, talent and even treasure. How we manage these relationships directly impacts our health and happiness. I once heard a man make a redundant statement that really is true: "Always keep the *main thing* the *main thing.*" Keeping the main thing the main thing requires a balancing act of sorts and requires making choices. How do we make good choices? By deciding what is most important to us.

Our personal lives could be divided into two areas; our *private* and *public lives.* If we are going to keep it all together we must find a way to balance these two.

Private Life

Our private lives bring fulfillment and happiness that can never come from anywhere else. This is a very important principle to remember. Our private lives are made up of three key relationships; our relationship with our family, our maker and ourselves. Happiness and contentment begins with being at peace with one's self. Finding personal time on a regular basis to do something you enjoy must be done on purpose and usually doesn't happen by accident. Good emotional and physical health directly impacts our other relationships. Sacrificing for others is noble, but failing to attend to one's personal needs will eventually have a negative impact on both our private and public lives.

Our family relationships must trump our public lives. This is also a very important principle to remember. We must order our lives in such a way that we make time for our spouses, children and parents. Unhappiness at home will translate into less effectiveness outside the home. Our families must know and believe that they are the more important than anything in our public lives. We demonstrate this when we give them our time, talent and treasure – in that order. They would much rather spend time with us than to have us spend money on them. Instead of talking about the things we bought for them as kids, my grown children mention far more often the times we took them fishing, bowling or to Chucky Cheese.

Public Life

Our public lives are made up of a number of key relationships also; our friends, our jobs, church family and others. More often than not, our public lives complicate our private lives. If we make our private lives a priority then it will help us better manage our public lives. If we are employed outside the home, there are certain demands that come with the job. We expect a certain amount of our time and talent to be devoted to the job. The Bible reminds us that we have a responsibility to take care of our family's needs. Adam actually had the first human job of *dressing & keeping* the Garden of Eden. So work is an honorable thing, but we must be careful not to allow work to become the dominant thing. Molding children and growing with a mate are far more important than making money.

We are created with a built in need for social

interaction with others. Friends, church family, community involvement and etc. are all important. They fulfill a need to be with people, contribute to society and make a difference in the lives of others. Involvement with others outside the home must be governed by what we realistically have time to do. That is also another great principle to remember. It's ok to say NO! No is sometimes the appropriate answer in some situations. One thing about it, you can never please all the people all the time so do what you feel in your heart is the best thing each time.
Practical Principles.

Here are a few helpful hints to remember in *Keeping it Together.*
1. Planning for work and play should be focused through the lens of personal priorities.
2. Our personal peace and contentment directly impacts other relationships.
3. Private life commitments should be considered first and take priority over public life.
4. Learn to say YES when you can and NO when you should.
5. Remember your children will be all grown up before you know it. Do *NOW* what you may have wished you had done later.
6. The greatest thing you can do for your children is to love your spouse. Make time for and work hard on making that a high priority.
7. The Scriptures remind us that one's close relationship our heavenly Father has a positive direct impact on our personal peace and contentment.
8. The Bible has a great book called Proverbs written by

a wise King named Solomon. It is one of the most practical works on keeping it all together that I've read. The book has 31 chapters and provides practical principles for private and public relationships. A great suggestion is to read one chapter each day using the day of the month as a guide and reading and extra chapter or two on the last day of the month with months that have less than 31 days. You might be surprised how much practical wisdom you'll find in just 31 short days.

Sometimes trying to *keep it all together* is like trying to drive a herd of cats, almost impossible. But if do our best to keep the *main thing* the *main thing* we might be amazed how the *other things* may fall into place.

Surviving the Lonely Holidays
Dr. Roy W. Harris

"How's she doing Doc?" I asked the doctor as he closed the door behind him in the Emergency Room. "She's not doing well," he said leaning back against the glass.

I could see Diana over his shoulder through the window. The doctor continued: *"She's developed a blood clot in the main artery that controls blood flow to her lower extremities."* I asked: *"What does that mean?"* He replied: *"There's nothing we can do. She's not going to make it."*

Arriving at these words on this day began three years ago with my wife's breast cancer diagnosis. Before the day ended, her battle with cancer was over. God sent his angel, who gently swept Diana up into his arms and carried her to her new home in heaven.

Fast-forward a few months. *Thanksgiving* and *Christmas*, two holidays that characterize the importance of family, would soon be here. For the first time my family and I would face these usually festive days with someone special missing.

The *Thanksgiving/Christmas/New Year* season can be very lonely and depressing for family members whose loved one has passed away. I remember well the first *Thanksgiving* and *Christmas* without my wife.

How can you survive those lonely holidays after you've lost someone you love?

There are a number of things I would suggest that might be helpful to you or someone you know get through those lonely, difficult days.

> *Remember and honor your loved one*. Do not avoid mentioning the parent, spouse, child, etc. Talking about them, calling their names and remembering may cause a tear or a smile. Both will be helpful with the grieving process for the whole family. Encourage family and friends to share stories and memories.

> *Reflect on the good things in your life*. Focus on the blessings God has sent your way. I think you'll find the good things far outweigh the painful ones. This may tip the scales of your life from loneliness to gratitude.

> *Reorganize holiday plans and traditions*. Do your holiday shopping early to reduce the stress. Your holiday traditions may have to be reorganized. Do not be afraid of deferring some traditions and beginning new ones.

> *Reach out to others*. Get out of the house! Staying secluded at home will make a difficult time even more difficult. Look for opportunities to invest in the lives of others during the holidays. This will help you take your eyes off self and focus beyond yourself. Get out there and get busy!

> *Reveal your feelings*. Share your feelings of loneliness with a close friend, confidant, pastor or another family member. Keeping them bottled up will pull you down further.

> *Remain physically and emotionally active*. Refrain from skipping meals or eating junk food. Eating a healthy diet and getting regular exercise will make you feel physically better and help you survive the emotional challenge of the holidays.

> *Remind yourself of the meanings of the season*. Thanksgiving is a time to be thankful. There are others who are not as blessed and are having life much harder than you. Thank God for all the good things he's brought into your life.

Christmas is a time of giving. Remind yourself of the great gift of his Son that God gave the world on that first *Christmas* morning. Also remind yourself of the great loss he suffered when his Son was murdered on the cross. Reflecting on the meaning of the season will help diminish the lonely feelings.

The holidays can be a lonely time, especially if you are grieving the loss of a loved one. Trying to avoid them will only make it worse.

I made it through that first holiday season and a number of holiday seasons since. Time was and is my friend and it will be yours too. With God's help, the help of friends and family, and your personal effort, you can and will overcome and survive the lonely holidays.

My prayer is that you enjoy a wonderful holiday season.

Surviving the Lonely Holidays

Dr. Roy W. Harris

"How's she doing Doc?" I asked the doctor as he closed the door behind him in the Emergency Room. *"She's not doing well,"* he said leaning back against the glass.

I could see Diana over his shoulder through the window. The doctor continued: *"She's developed a blood clot in the main artery that controls blood flow to her lower extremities."* I asked: *"What does that mean?"* He replied: *"There's nothing we can do. She's not going to make it."*

Arriving at these words on this day began three years ago with my wife's breast cancer diagnosis. Before the day ended, her battle with cancer was over. God sent his angel, who gently swept Diana up into his arms and carried her to her new home in heaven.

Fast-forward a few months. *Thanksgiving* and *Christmas*, two holidays that characterize the importance of family, would soon be here. For the first time my family and I would face these usually festive days with someone special missing.

The *Thanksgiving/Christmas/New Year* season can be very lonely and depressing for family members whose loved one has passed away. I remember well the first *Thanksgiving* and *Christmas* without my wife.

How can you survive those lonely holidays after

you've lost someone you love?

There are a number of things I would suggest that might be helpful to you or someone you know get through those lonely, difficult days.

➢ *Remember and honor your loved one.* Do not avoid mentioning the parent, spouse, child, etc. Talking about them, calling their names and remembering may cause a tear or a smile. Both will be helpful with the grieving process for the whole family. Encourage family and friends to share stories and memories.

➢ *Reflect on the good things in your life.* Focus on the blessings God has sent your way. I think you'll find the good things far outweigh the painful ones. This may tip the scales of your life from loneliness to gratitude.

➢ *Reorganize holiday plans and traditions.* Do your holiday shopping early to reduce the stress. Your holiday traditions may have to be reorganized. Do not be afraid of deferring some traditions and beginning new ones.

➢ *Reach out to others.* Get out of the house! Staying secluded at home will make a difficult time even more difficult. Look for opportunities to invest in the lives of others during the holidays. This will help you take your eyes off self and focus beyond yourself. Get out there and get busy!

➢ *Reveal your feelings.* Share your feelings of loneliness with a close friend, confidant, pastor or another family member. Keeping them bottled up will pull you down further.

➢ *Remain physically and emotionally active.* Refrain

from skipping meals or eating junk food. Eating a healthy diet and getting regular exercise will make you feel physically better and help you survive the emotional challenge of the holidays.

➢ *Remind yourself of the meanings of the season.* *Thanksgiving* is a time to be thankful. There are others who are not as blessed and are having life much harder than you. Thank God for all the good things he's brought into your life.

Christmas is a time of giving. Remind yourself of the great gift of his Son that God gave the world on that first *Christmas* morning. Also remind yourself of the great loss he suffered when his Son died. Reflecting on the meaning of the season will help diminish the lonely feelings.

The holidays can be a lonely time, especially if you are grieving the loss of a loved one. Trying to avoid them will only make it worse.

I made it through that first holiday season and a number of holiday seasons since. Time was and is my friend and it will be yours too. With God's help, the help of friends and family, and your personal effort, you can and will overcome and survive the lonely holidays.

My prayer is that you enjoy a wonderful Thanksgiving, a Merry Christmas or a Blessed Hanukah, and a Happy New Year.

Congratulations on our Anniversary

By ROY W. HARRIS

A wise man will make sure he doesn't forget two very important dates; his wife's birthday and his anniversary.

Anniversaries are celebrations commemorating the annually recurring date of a past event, of historical, national or personal importance (according to The Free Dictionary by Farlex). Wow, that's quite a mouthful, but we all have anniversaries that are important to us. In this issue of Wilson Living we are celebrating the anniversary of the successful launch of the magazine some three years ago. Congratulations Angel and Becky and to all those who've worked hard to produce a top shelf magazine that is a credit to Wilson County and an asset to Middle Tennessee.

In reality, we celebrate a variety of anniversaries. A lady reminded me this past Sunday that she and her husband were celebrating the first anniversary of their baptisms and that I was the minister who performed the baptisms one year ago. This was an important personal occasion for them. Birthdays are also anniversaries celebrating our births and the births of those we love and cherish.

This time of the year also reminds us of a couple of events that occur annually. We celebrate Thanksgiving and Christmas. Thanksgiving is truly a unique and special holiday with Christmas following right on its' heels. Thanksgiving and Christmas are highlighted by family, food and fun all wrapped up in symbols of the holiday season, symphonies of holiday song and somber reflection of the past year's goodness and blessings.

I recently returned from a visit to the Middle East and was once again reminded of a number of the blessings that we sometimes take for granted. Just like at Christmas time when we are blessed to receive special gifts from those who love us, we Tennesseans have been blessed by our heavenly Father with many national gifts. We are blessed to live in peace. Even though we've suffered war and tragedy at times, we live in the safest country in the world. We are blessed with the freedom to worship openly or ship at all if we so choose. W with the freedom to speak our m fear of reprisal. We are blessed the highest standards of living in

While in the Middle East I Bedouin boy in the desert on the of the Jordan River near the Dea ing a flock of sheep and goat crouched down in the hot sun lief in the shade of the only bu the area. We had just passed the of his family and friends in ou conditioned bus. I was reminded blessed we are. We are blessed ning water. The Bedouins drew t

Congratulations on Your Anniversary!

By Roy W. Harris

A wise man will make sure he doesn't forget two very important dates; his *wife's birthday* and his *anniversary*.

Anniversaries are celebrations commemorating the annually recurring date of a past event, of historical, national or personal importance (according to The Free Dictionary by Farlex). Wow, that's quite a mouthful but we all have anniversaries that are important to us. In this issue of *Wilson Living* we are celebrating the anniversary of the successful launch of the magazine some three years ago. Congratulations Angel and Becky and to all those who've worked hard to produce a *top shelf* magazine that is a credit to Wilson County and an asset to Middle Tennessee.

In reality, we celebrate a variety of *anniversaries*. A lady reminded me this past Sunday that she and her husband were celebrating the first anniversary of their baptisms and that I was the minister who performed the baptisms one year ago. This was an important personal occasion for them. Birthdays are also *anniversaries* celebrating our births and the births of those we love and cherish.

This time of the year also reminds us of a couple of events that occur annually. We celebrate

Thanksgiving and *Christmas.* Thanksgiving is truly a unique and special holiday with Christmas following right on its' heels. Thanksgiving and Christmas are highlighted by family, food and fun all wrapped up in symbols of the holiday season, symphonies of holiday song and somber reflection of the past year's goodness and blessings.

I recently returned from a visit to the Middle East and was once again reminded of a number of the blessings that we sometimes *take* for granted. Just like at Christmas time when we are blessed to receive special gifts from those who love us, we Tennesseans have been blessed by our heavenly Father with many national gifts. We are blessed to live in *peace.* Even though we've suffered war and tragedy at times, we live in the safest country in the world. We are blessed with the *freedom to worship* openly or not to worship at all if we so choose. We are blessed with the *freedom* to speak our minds without fear of reprisal. We are blessed with one of the highest *standards of living* in the world.

While in the Middle East I observed a Bedouin boy in the desert on the West Bank of the Jordan River near the Dead Sea herding a flock of sheep and goats. He was crouched down in the hot sun seeking relief in the shade of the only bush I saw in the area.

We had just passed the tent camp of his family and friends in our cool air-conditioned bus. I was reminded of just how blessed we are. We are blessed with *running water*. The Bedouins drew theirs from a tanker that had been trucked in from miles away. One out of three people in the world do not have adequate sanitation facilities and over one billion do not have safe water to drink. We are blessed with *food*. We all have our Thanksgiving and Christmas favorites. One out of six people in the world go to bed hungry every night. We are blessed with *warm and dry places* to live. The average American home or apartment is considered to be homes of the very wealthy by most of the rest of the world. We are blessed with *warm clothes* to fend off the winter cold. *Water, food, shelter* and *clothing,* the necessities of life – we have them all.

As we celebrate the 390th anniversary of the first Pilgrims' Thanksgiving celebration in Plymouth, Massachusetts and the approximately 2000th year anniversary of the birth of Christ in Bethlehem maybe it would be wise for us reflect a moment. The holy scriptures teach us *that every good and perfect gift comes from above, given to us by our heavenly Father.* Thanksgiving and Christmas should be times for family, food and fun; but may I suggest one more thing?

When we gather around the table and Christmas tree, let us take a moment to recount our personal and family blessings, remind the next generation where our blessings came from and resolve to reach out and share those blessings with others. The scriptures also remind us that God blesses those who help others that are truly in need. The Lord said; *I was hungry and you gave me something to eat, I was thirsty and you gave me something to drink, I was a stranger and you invited me in, I needed clothes and you clothed me, I was sick and you looked after me, I was in prison and you came to visit me.* When He was asked; when did we do these things? He reminded them that every act of kindness to others was an act of kindness to Him.

There are several worthy non-profit organizations in our community whose business is lending a helping hand to those in need. Why not adopt one this holiday season and share part of the bounty of blessings that God has sent your way? It would be a nice way to celebrate two great anniversaries and pass the precious gift of giving down to a new generation. *Congratulations* Wilson Living Magazine. *Happy Thanksgiving* and *Merry Christmas* everyone!

Reflections

Eventide

Sunrise on the ocean near Myrtle Beach, SC
Photo by Roy's brother, Ric

By ROY HARRIS

Ah… the ocean.

There is a special peace that comes with the sun slowly rising from the sea with its beams of light growing brighter and brighter as it breaks free from the horizon and begins its' course across the eastern sky. It reminds us that, just as the sun rises anew every morning, each day brings new opportunities to begin again.

The ocean can be a wonderful teacher. The tide comes in and the tide goes out. High tide and low tide peak twice each day and never at the same time. Most tides are predictable. Local television news and weather reports often list the tidal schedules for coastal cities and beaches. The tides can also be unpredictable, impacted by wind and storms. Hurricanes often turn gentle lapping waves into fast moving, huge destructive walls of water which can destroy property and unprotected lives.

Life is, in many ways, like the ocean.

Every person is unique, special and important and is created by God with a purpose for his or her life. Our lives begin like low tide ever moving forward, a day at a time, until finally reaching its' zenith, our own individual high tides. As we age, life begins to relinquish the

Roy with one of his King Mackerel off the coast near Murrell's Inlet, SC

strides forward which we've achieved, and we move ever closer to changing our residence from this world to the next, returning to God who created us.

There is a certain wealth and beauty on the incoming tide. Most avid salt water fishermen (of which I like to be included) will agree that the incoming tide brings with it the wealth of the sea, the beauty of the blue green water, the clean salt air and the calming beat of the breaking waves. The best surf fishing experience comes with the incoming tide - (wading into waist deep water and casting your bait or lure into the approaching waves). The tide brings with it bait fish and shrimp which attract larger game fish. This bodes well for a great day on the water and hopefully for the fisherman's supper table also.

The beach, scarred from a day of flying Frisbees, errant footballs, bright colored beach umbrellas and low riding beach chairs, is cleansed with the white foam of the incoming tide. As the tide reaches its' highest point, the serenity of the scene is so calming and peaceful. The slowly receding tide reveals a clean slate ready for the next round of sun worshipers, surf fish-

Eventide

Dr. Roy W. Harris

Ah…. the ocean. There is a special peace that comes with the sun slowly rising from the sea with its beams of light growing brighter and brighter as it breaks free from the horizon and begins its' course across the eastern sky. It reminds us that, just as the sun rises anew every morning, each day brings new opportunities to begin again.

The ocean can be a wonderful teacher. The tide comes in and the tide goes out. High tide and low tide peek twice each day and never at the same time. Most tides are predictable. Local television news and weather reports often list the tidal schedules for coastal cities and beaches. The tides can also be unpredictable, impacted by wind and storms. Hurricanes often turn gentle lapping waves into fast moving huge destructive walls of water, which can destroy property and unprotected lives.

Life is in many ways like the ocean. Every person is a unique, special and important and is created by God with a purpose for his/her life. Our lives begin like low tide ever moving forward a day at a time until finally reaching its' zenith, our own individual high tides. As we age, life begins to relinquish the strides forward which we've achieved and we move ever closer to changing our residence from this world to the next, returning to God who created us.

There is a certain wealth and beauty on the incoming tide. Most avid salt-water fishermen (of which I like to be included) will agree that the incoming tide brings with it the wealth of the sea, the beauty of the blue green water, the clean salt air and the calming beat of the breaking waves. The best surf fishing experience comes with the incoming tide - (wading into waist deep water and casting your bait or lure into the approaching waves). The tide brings with it bait fish and shrimp which attract larger game fish. This bodes well for a great day on the water and hopefully for the fisherman's supper table also.

The beach, scarred from a day of flying Frisbees, errant footballs, bright colored beach umbrellas and low riding beach chairs, is cleansed with the white foam of the incoming tide. As the tide reaches its' highest point, the serenity of scene is so calming and peaceful. The slowly reseeding tide reveals a *clean slate* ready for the next round of sun worshipers, surf fishermen, sandcastle architects, shell collectors and adventure seeking children.

The *journey of life* is a series of ups and downs much like the tides. Rising and falling as though on a prescribed timetable and set course. We all have our share of missteps and sometimes even suffer great tragedies and disappointments. The death of a family member, failing health, the loss of a job, passed over for a promotion, turned down for a loan, the washing machine quits or the car won't start are only a few of the things that can happen on a given day. But life is also filled with great joy and happiness. Falling in love, getting that *big break*, the birth of a child or grandchild, moving into one's first home etc. bring *the good feelings* that we all enjoy and are the kinds of things we would rather experience.

So how do we balance life's ups and downs and the events that we have little control over? Having the right perspective can help keep life from overwhelming us. Just as surely as the tide goes out, it will come in again. Every day is like the tide and with each new day comes new opportunities to start fresh. The setting of yesterday's sun helps wash away some of life's missteps, mistakes and heartbreaks. Just as the sunrise brings a new day, we can rise each morning striving to live life *one day at a time.* This is a great way to balance those *joys* and *setbacks.* The *only* day we really have is *today*. We cannot relive yesterday and tomorrow will never come. When we wake up tomorrow, next week or next year, it will *always* be *today*.

Learning to live *one day at a time* helps us in so many ways. It frees us from the stress of *worrying* about tomorrow or trying to *second-guess* our decisions from yesterday. The scriptures tell us: "*do not worry about tomorrow, for tomorrow will worry about itself. Each day has enough trouble of its own.*" So you see…. you don't even have to take my word for it. The good LORD himself tells us the best way to do life is *one day at a time.* Take heart, just as surely as the tide goes out it will come back in again. You may have some difficult times today, but rest assured there are better days ahead. When you need a bit of encouragement, look to the beauty of the ocean and wonder of the sea. Leave the past behind you and try not to worry about the future. Do you your best to live life today, ONE DAY AT A TIME.

Vacation Time

Reflections
by Roy Harris

Roy is a national Conference, Seminar and Retreat speaker and can be contacted at Roy@royharris.info or view his website at www.royharris.info

It's 7 a.m., and I'm sitting on the balcony with a view that's unbelievable. There's a steady breeze from the ocean, and the salt air is so refreshing early in the morning. I just watched the sun like a fireball being reborn perform its daily routine of slowly rising from the depths of the ocean. I'm on the 3rd floor balcony of our in-laws' condo at Wrightsville Beach, North Carolina looking out over the expanse of the beautiful Atlantic Ocean. Amy and I are looking forward to a week of fun, sun, surf fishing, seafood, spending time with family and just plain enjoying some time off.

Have you ever thought about why we enjoy vacation time so much?

I'm sure there are a variety of answers one might give. We are creatures of habit. We really do love routine. We have our Monday through Friday morning routines and our Saturday and Sunday routines. When we eat out we usually don't need a menu because we know what we want before we sit down at our favorite restaurants. We like to park at about the same place at church, and Heaven help us if someone is sitting in our seats when we get inside. It throws our whole worship experience off (ha). The routine of life brings with it pressure and stress. It's not easy juggling all the responsibilities of being a good parent, fulfilling the demands placed on us at work, giving our spouses the attention they need and deserve and finding time for one's self.

I'm a big fan of vacations. Vacation time provides an opportunity to get away from much of the stress of daily routine we are accustomed to. A change of scenery, a few days away from work, activities which involve the whole family, a walk on the beach holding your spouse's hand or just sitting in a rocking chair on the porch watching the sunset over the Smoky Mountains can do wonders for us. If we do it right, we can return home refreshed and ready to tackle the routine of life again.

Have you ever said or thought while on vacation I'd love to do this all the time?

Well, we all know that is not usually possible. What makes vacations so special is that we can't do them all the time. That brings us back to the routine of life and the pressure and stress which goes with it. There are some practi... can do to help r... pressure and he... day in and day... life. I'm certain... but I know a sou... source is God's W...

Here are some helpful hints from the heavenly book.

Remind yourself that you are unique and special. God kne... fore you were born and has a special life plan for you. (Psalm... gerprints suggested it, and DNA confirms it. You are unique. T... another human being on earth exactly like you. God knows you... everything about you.

Try to live life one day at a time. (Proverbs 21:1) Too many... to either live in the past or the future. Just a reminder of somet... ready know - you can only live life today. Yesterday is gone and... return. It may be relived in our minds from time to time, but we... in the past. We should learn from our past mistakes but remem... not only forgives, but He also forgets. We should seek to do t... cannot live in the future. When tomorrow comes, it will alwa... Don't borrow from tomorrow's trouble and problems. It pro... turn out to be as bad as you thought it might anyway. AKA – ... over the past or the future. Take on life with its blessings and... day.

Don't spend too much time thinking about the things you... anything about. (Proverbs 3:5) There are some things that we... change. We wish we could. We wish it could be different, but... Wishing and fretting will only increase pressure and stress. S... must be turned over the Lord. He's big enough to handle the... can't.

Do your best and let God do the rest. (Proverbs 3:3-4,6) I'm a... ment of the principle that hard work and doing the right thing pay... end. Proverbs reminds us that if we love people and are faithful a... of life, then we will gain favor and a good name among others... spect of God Himself. Doing the right thing is always the right thi... Many other things could be said about, eating right, getting ple... exercising regularly, but I don't what to throw at you and add m... (ha). But we know those things contribute to our ability to handle... of life.

We are in the middle of summer vacation season. Take it litt... and vacate the premises. You don't have to travel a long dist... home, but you might be surprised what a few days away will do fo... your family. Remember when you get back home, God can help... the pressure and stress of l...

242

VACATION TIME

By
Roy W. Harris

7:00 a.m. and I'm sitting on the balcony with a view that's unbelievable. There's a steady breeze from the ocean and the salt air is so refreshing early in the morning. I just watched the sun like a fireball being reborn perform its' daily routine of slowly rising from the depths of the ocean. I'm on the 3rd floor balcony of our in-laws' condo at Wrightsville Beach, NC looking out over the expanse of the beautiful Atlantic Ocean. Amy & I are looking forward to a week of fun, sun, serf fishing, seafood, spending time with family and just plain enjoying some time off.

Have you ever thought about why we enjoy vacation time so much?

I'm sure there are a variety of answers one might give. We are creatures of habit. We really do love routine. We have our Monday through Friday morning routines and our Saturday and Sunday routines. When we eat out we usually don't need a menu because we know what we want before we sit down at our favorite restaurants. We like to park at about the same place at church and heaven help us if someone is sitting in *our seats* when we get inside. It throws our whole worship experience off (ha). The routine of life brings with it pressure and stress. It's not easy juggling all the responsibilities of being a good parent, fulfilling the demands placed on us at work, giving our spouses the attention they need and deserve and finding time for one's self.

I'm a big fan of vacations. Vacation time provides an opportunity to *get away* from much of the stress of daily routine we are accustomed to. A change of scenery, a few days away from work, activities which involve the whole family, a walk on the beach holding your spouse's hand or just sitting in a rocking chair on the porch watching the sunset over the Smoky Mountains can do wonders for us. If we do it right, we can return home refreshed and ready to tackle the routine of life again.

Have you ever said or thought while on vacation I'd love to do this all the time?

Well, we all know that is not usually possible. What makes vacations so special is that we can't do them all the time. That brings us back to the routine of life and the pressure and stress that goes with it. There are some practical things we can do to help relieve stress and pressure and better enjoy the day in and day out routine of life. I'm certainly not an expert but I know a source that is. That source is God's Word.

Here are some helpful hints from the heavenly book.

1. *Remind yourself that you are unique and special.* God knew you before you were born and has a special life plan for you. (Psalm 139). Fingerprints suggested it and DNA confirms it. You are unique. There is not another human being on earth exactly like you. God knows your name and everything about you.
2. *Try to live life one day at a time.* (Proverbs 21:1) Too

many people try to either live in the past or the future. Just a reminder of something you already know. You can only live life today. Yesterday is gone and can never return. It may be relived in our minds from time to time, but we cannot live in the past. We should learn from our past mistakes but remember that God not only forgives, but He also forgets. We should seek to do the same. We cannot live in the future. When tomorrow comes, it will always be today. Don't borrow from tomorrow's trouble and problems. It probably won't turn out to be as bad as you thought it might anyway. AKA – Don't stress over the past or the future. Take on life with its blessings and problems today.
3. *Don't spend too much time thinking about the things you cannot do anything about.* (Proverbs 3:5) There are some things that we just cannot change. We wish we could. We wish it could be different, but it just isn't. Wishing and fretting will only increase pressure and stress. Some things must be turned over the Lord. He's big enough to handle the things we can't.
4. *Do your best and let God do the rest.* (Proverbs 3:3-4,6) I'm a big proponent of the principle that hard work and doing the right thing pays off in the end. Proverbs reminds us that if we love people and are faithful at the tasks of life, then we will gain favor and a good name among others and the respect of God Himself. Doing the right thing is always the right thing to do.

Many other things could be said about, eating right, getting plenty of rest, exercising regularly but I don't what to throw at you and add more stress (ha). But we know those things contribute to our ability to handle the issues of life.

We are in the middle of summer vacation season.

Take a little time off and *vacate the premises*. You don't have to travel a long distance from home, but you might be surprised what a few days away will do for you and your family. Remember when you get back home, God can help you with the pressure and stress of life. Take it from God – He's an expert.

Reflections

THE END
of Summer

Labor Day is known as a day to recognize the dedication and hard work of all those who labor but also the symbolic end of summer to most Tennesseans

By ROY W. HARRIS

Wow – where did the summer go? I think we all feel that way when the reality of Fall begins to set in with arrival of the Labor Day weekend. The tradition of celebrating Labor Day has a history spanning approximately 120 years. It became an official national holiday in 1894 during President Grover Cleveland's administration. The bill took only six days to make it through both houses of Congress and to the President's desk.

Labor Day

Labor Day has come to symbolize much more in our modern world than its original purpose of recognizing the dedication and hard work of those whose labor helps make our country strong. Labor Day is the symbolic end of summer to most Tennesseans. This is also the time of year that many sports fans have been waiting for. College football teams in the National Collegiate Athletic Association usually play their first games the week before Labor Day. The National Football League usually plays its first game on the Thursday following Labor Day. Let's not forget another biggie which impacts all of us. To stay in style, Labor Day is the last day when it is permissible to wear white until Memorial Day weekend rolls around at the end of May (ha).

In a previous issue of *Wilson Living*, I extolled the wonderful benefits of *Vacation Time*. Work also has great value. Work is nothing new and is part of all our lives. We'd rather play than work ... or would we? The first mention of work and our involvement in it is found in the very first book of the bible, the book of Genesis (which literally means book of beginnings.) Most of us are familiar with the biblical

The End of Summer

By ROY W. HARRIS

Labor Day is known as a day to recognize the dedication and hard work of all those who labor but also the symbolic end of summer to most Tennesseans

Wow – where did the summer go? I think we all feel that way when the reality of Fall begins to set in with arrival of the Labor Day weekend.

The tradition of celebrating Labor Day has a history spanning approximately 120 years. It became an official national holiday in 1894 during President Grover Cleveland's administration. The bill took only six days to make it through both houses of Congress and to the President's desk.

Labor Day

Labor Day has come to symbolize much more in our modern world than its original purpose of recognizing the dedication and hard work of those whose labor helps make our country strong. Labor Day is the symbolic end of summer to most Tennesseans. This is also the time of year that many sports fans have been waiting for. College football teams in the National Collegiate Athletic Association usually play their first games the week before Labor Day. The National Football League usually plays its first game on the Thursday following Labor Day. Let's not forget another biggie that impacts all of us. To stay in style, Labor Day is the last day when it is permissible to wear white until Memorial Day weekend roles around at the end of May (ha).

In a previous issue of Wilson Living, I extolled the wonderful benefits of Vacation Time. Work also has great value. Work is nothing new and is part of all our lives.

We'd rather play than work ... or would we? The first mention of work and our involvement in it is found in the very first book of the bible, the book of Genesis (which literally means book of beginnings.)

Most of us are familiar with the biblical story of Adam and Eve created by God and placed in the Garden of Eden. We have seen the commercials of Adam being tempted to eat the forbidden apple and the idea that paradise provided freedom from many things including work.

If you look at that story a little more closely I think you'll find something very interesting. God provided a wonderful environment in the garden but he assigned man the responsibility to work and take care of it. The bible basically says that God placed Adam in the Garden of Eden not only to enjoy the benefits of paradise but also to work in and take care of the garden.

Spring and summer weather in middle Tennessee seemed to be a bit unusual this year. A warmer than normal winter gave way to a searing hot and dry June followed by a wet July. I was truly amazed when lawns turned brown prematurely and plants, shrubs and small trees struggled to survive. Even more amazing was the transformation the July rains brought with an exceptionally green August. Gardens that seemed to be doomed in June not only survived but also thrived by the end of July.

Reflections

Grieving with Hope
BY DR. ROY W. HARRIS, PH.D.

Life was good. The kids were grown and the empty nest was even better than we'd imagined. Then came my wife's terminal illness followed by her treatments, our times of hope, our setbacks then ultimately the death of my best friend. After thirty-three years of happy marriage, two children and three grandchildren, how could it come to this?

Isn't it amazing how our lives can be forever changed in a moment? It may arrive like a slow moving shadow or suddenly like a streak of lightening in the night sky. However it appears, it always brings emptiness and emotional pain. We pray believing that God has the power to heal. God may choose not to heal and our loved ones die. We hurt deep within. Sometimes we become angry. We do not understand why this has happened to us and our loved ones. Then the grief begins. Grieving is not an enjoyable experience, but one that is needed and healthy.

Grieving is OK

One of the most important things to remember when we lose a loved one is that it's OK to grieve. As a matter of fact it is more than OK, it is normal and healthy. Some make the mistake of not admitting their pain and hurt and carry the deep wound much longer than God wants us to. That's a big mistake. There's no set way one should grieve or time frame of how long. But there is a timeline for grief. Grief has a beginning and there is an end out there somewhere. Does that mean we should forget those loved ones? Absolutely not! Does it mean we should get over losing them? Not necessarily. It does mean that we have to go on living. We may never completely get over the death of a loved one but we can and must learn to live with it. Understanding that there are periods of grief we pass through and recognizing where you might be in the grieving process.

* Initial shock when you lose a loved one is the first period of grief. This could last from a few minutes after your loved one dies, it may last several hours and it could last for days. There are several emotions you might feel. One is false guilt. Another is false blame, blaming other family members, medical personnel and even God himself for not doing more to help or save your loved one.

* The second period of grief begins with our lives becoming disorganized. This could last for several weeks or months. This is the time when your lifestyle is forced to change. Hasty decisions and rash statements of what you will or won't do should be avoided. Too many people make the mistake of sacrificing future happiness on an unneeded sense of loyalty to the past. Our loved ones wouldn't want us to remain unhappy and grieve for them the rest of our lives. Reminders of the past have a way of surfacing and there may be some confessing to God and others because of actions and words spoken in shock or anger.

* The third period of grief begins with a conscious decision to reorganize our lives and move on. I remember clearly about nine months after my wife's passing, on our anniversary I laid two dozen roses on her grave. I didn't hear an audible voice but God spoke to my heart as I wept at her graveside. He reminded me that just as he had a plan for my wife's life he also had one for mine. He had more work for me to do and it was time for me to move forward with his will for my life. I walked away from her grave that day leaving some of the pain and sorrow with a change of heart.

There is Help!

The word of God is a tremendous comfort. Deuteronomy 31:9 reminds us that God is with us at all times. We do not have to bear the burden of grief alone according to Psalm 23:4. According to Psalm 68:19, God feels our pain and bears our sorrow. We should also look to our church family for strength and encouragement. When friends offer help or invite us to be part of their lives, we should see this as one way God is seeking to begin filling an empty void in our own lives. Learn to say yes and thank you.

There is Hope!

Hope begins with recognition of where we are with our grief. We must grieve and others cannot tell us how we should do it or how long our grief should last. One thing's for sure. Our grief must be a means to an end. Our goal should be to allow God to help us put the pieces back together and move forward with our lives. We must ask the Lord to help us and give us the wisdom and strength to press on. We should take positive steps to move forward. We shouldn't preserve our homes as monuments to our deceased loved ones. Consider cleaning out closets, rearranging rooms and donating clothes to Goodwill or passing them along to others who will get use and enjoyment from them. You may want to consider downsizing and moving to a home with less upkeep and maintenance. It's time to reorganize.

A Final Word

If you're in the midst of grieving, I have great news. THERE IS HOPE. I'm a few years removed from the loss of my wife. God's gentle hand has led me forward. He led a fine Christian lady into my life and the sunshine of happiness has returned. I am a living testimony of the fact that you not only can live through it but you can live beyond it. God's plan for you is certain and his will is perfect. The

Living Beyond Grief

By Roy W. Harris

Life was good. The kids were grown and the empty nest was even better than we'd imagined it could be. Then came my wife's terminal illness followed by her treatments, our times of hope, our setbacks then ultimately the death of my best friend. After thirty-three years of happy marriage, two children and three grandchildren, how could it come to this? Isn't it amazing how our lives can be forever changed in a moment? Our hopes and dreams can be turned into hurt and disappointment. Death is never easy. It may arrive like a slow moving shadow or suddenly like a streak of lightening in the night sky. However it appears, it always brings emptiness and emotional pain.

One of the classic stories in the bible is the death of Jesus' good friend Lazarus found in John 11. It contains one of the best descriptions of illness, prayer for healing, God's decision not to heal and the death of a loved one. Mary and Martha are overcome with grief. Jesus feels their pain. Lazarus is raised from the dead. This is a perfect illustration of what we may face one day. Our loved ones become ill. We pray knowing that God has the power to heal. God may choose not to heal and our loved ones die. We hurt deep within. Sometimes we become angry. We do not understand why this has happened to our loved ones and us. Then the grief begins. Grieving is not an enjoyable experience, but one that is needed and healthy.

Death Becomes Real.

There are a couple of times when the reality of death seems to take center stage. The first is the year immediately following the death of a loved. That year is filled with all the *firsts*; the *first* time sitting alone at church, the *first* night with a child's empty bed, the *first* birthday of the absent loved one, the *first* anniversary without your spouse, the *first* week alone in an empty house are only a few *firsts* that we may experience during that first year. A second time that can be difficult is the holidays. Both of my dad's parents passed away on the same date about twenty years apart. My grandfather died on the day before Thanksgiving and my grandmother on Thanksgiving Day. Thanksgiving holds a special place in the life of our family. For many years now my brother and I have made a point to be at mom and dad's house for Thanksgiving Day. I remember well the first Thanksgiving after my wife's passing. It was a strange feeling sitting at mom's dining room table with one very conspicuous empty chair. I ate the wonderful meal mom had prepared but I was a bit preoccupied with that empty chair next to me reminding me of the empty place in my heart.

Death's impact seems to march front and center during the holidays. Christmas was a special time at our house. My wife would decorate to no end! We built a new home during her illness to give her something to plan for and look forward to. The house was completed during the early part of the second year of her three-year illness. She now had a large two-story house and one of her great joys was to make it a Christmas winter wonderland. After she passed away, it was just not the same. I pulled out a fraction of the decorations and did the best I could to make it an enjoyable time for the children and grandchildren, but my heart was just not in it. We still carried on our family Christmas traditions but somehow they were not the same. Something was missing and that something was someone. Christmas was a difficult emotional time.

Grieving is OK.

One of the most important things to remember when we lose a loved one is that it's OK to grieve. As a matter of fact it is more than OK, it is normal and healthy. Some make the mistake of not admitting their pain and hurt and carry the deep wound much longer than God wants us to. That's a big mistake. There's no set way one should grieve or time frame of how long. But there is a timeline for grief. Grief has a beginning and there is an end out there somewhere. Does that mean we should forget those loved ones? Absolutely not! Does it mean we should get over losing them? Not necessarily. It does mean that we have to go on living. We may never completely get over the death of a loved one but we can and must learn to live with it. How can one do that you might ask? One of the keys is understanding that there are periods of grief we pass through and recognizing where you might be in the grieving process.

- ***Initial shock*** when you lose a loved one is the

first period of grief. This could last from a few minutes after your loved one dies, it may last several hours and it could last for days. There are several emotions you might feel. One is *false guilt.* You wish you'd done something different or done more. Another is *false blame*, blaming other family members, medical personnel and even God himself for not doing more to help or save your loved one. *Anger* is another emotion that sometimes shows up in the early hours of grief. *Fear* of the future can paralyze you.

- After the initial shock, the *second period* of grief begins with our lives becoming **disorganized**. This could last for several weeks or months. The old routines and patterns of life are left in shambles. This is the time when your lifestyle is forced to change. Hasty decisions and rash statements of what you will or won't do should be avoided .Too many people make the mistake of sacrificing future happiness on an unneeded sense of loyalty to the past. Our loved ones wouldn't want us to remain unhappy and grieve for them the rest of our lives. Reminders of the past have a way of surfacing and there may be some confessing to God and others because of actions and words spoken in shock or anger.

- The *third period* of grief begins with a conscious decision to **reorganize** our lives and move on. I remember clearly about nine months after my wife's passing. On our anniversary I laid two-dozen roses on her grave. I didn't hear an audible voice but God spoke to my heart as I wept at her graveside. He reminded me that just as he had a plan for my wife's life he also had one for mine. He had more work for me to do and it was time for me to move forward with his will for my life. I walked away from her grave that day leaving some of the pain and sorrow with a change of heart.

There is Help!

The word of God is a tremendous comfort. Deuteronomy 31:9 reminds us that God is with us at all times. We do not have to bear the burden of grief alone according to Psalm 23:4. According to Psalm 68:19, God feels our pain and bears our sorrow. He understands the hurt of losing a loved one and supplies the salve that heals our wounded souls in Psalm 147:3. Remember, Romans 8:28's lesson that everything that happens to us in the long run is for our good and his glory. We should also look to our church family for strength and encouragement. When friends offer help or invite us to be part of their lives, we should see this as one-way God is seeking to begin filling an empty void in our own lives. Learn to say yes and thank you.

There is Hope!

After hearing the voice of the Lord urging me to move forward and making the decision to try and do just that, my life began to change. The deep pain, sorrow and loneliness didn't go away overnight, but I began to realize that there was a light at the end of this dark tunnel. There was a glimmer of sunlight beginning to pierce through the dense fog I'd been in for so long.

Hope begins with recognition of where we are with our grief. We must grieve and others cannot tell us how we should do it or how long our grief should last. One thing's for sure. Our grief must be a means to an end. Our goal should be to allow God to help us put the pieces back together and move forward with our lives. We must ask the Lord to help us and give us the wisdom and strength to press on. We should take positive steps to move forward. We shouldn't preserve our homes as monuments to our deceased loved ones. Consider cleaning out closets, rearranging rooms and donating clothes to Good Will or passing them along to others who will get use and enjoyment from them. You may want to consider downsizing and moving to a home with less upkeep and maintenance. It's time to reorganize.

A Final Word

If you're in the midst of grieving, I have great news. THERE IS HOPE. I'm a few years removed from the loss of my wife. God's gentle hand has led me forward. He led a fine Christian lady into my life and the sunshine of happiness has returned. I am a living testimony of the fact that you not only can live through this, but you can live beyond it. God's plan for you is certain and his will is perfect. There is a great *life* waiting for you just *beyond* your *grief.*

TAG, you're It!

by ROY W. HARRIS

Simon Says, raise your right hand! Red Rover Red Rover send Billy over! Simon Says and Red Rover are a couple of childhood games that we fondly remember playing especially with cousins. What in the world do kid games have to do with adult lives and the year 2012? Then there is that the other game called hide and seek. It was always more fun to be the hider rather than the seeker. Ready or not here I come were those key words that alerted all of us hiders that the seeker was on the way. Well, ready or not a New Year is not just on the way, it has already arrived. They seem to slip up on us sooner each year.

The book is now closed on 2011. But the good news is that 2012 brings with it great opportunities. You can close the chapters of failure and shortcomings of last year. That weight you wanted to lose, that project you wanted to start, those words you wish you'd said are all now in the past. It's almost like a chalk or marker board in school. When the teacher finishes one lesson he/she removes all evidence of it and moves on to the next.

2012 will add another volume to the books which make up our lives. The writing of it has already begun. It will contain multiple chapters with a variety of subjects; personal life, family relationships, work obligations, service to God and church and service to the community to name a few. There are some things that might be wise for us to keep in mind. One way to do this is to ask ourselves a couple of questions:

What are some specific things I'd like to accomplish this coming year? Many times things come up over and over again that we know need to be done. But somehow at the end of the year they still remain unfinished. Taking a few minutes in this first month of the year to jot down a to do list of things to be accomplished in 2012 can be a great way to organize your thoughts in a tangible way and will be a good starting point.

What is the most important thing I want to get done this year? Choosing the most important thing on the list is a great place to begin. Make it the top priority.

What should be the most important things on our lists for 2012? That's a great question! I believe we can never go wrong by remembering some principles designed to help guide us in determining the priorities of life. We have only to reflect upon the earliest form of spiritual guidelines, the Ten Commandments to find a successful model that has proven itself through the centuries. The summary of those commandments teach us to place God first, others second and ourselves last.

What about ourselves? A man named Paul who penned a majority of the words in the New Testament of the Bible has some very good advice. He said something like this: I haven't accomplished all I'd like to yet, but I've put the past behind me and I'm looking ahead to the future. I've set a goal and now I'm working to accomplish it. I have confidence that I will succeed in the end (Philippians 4:13-14). This is great advice for us today. So what if you didn't accomplish all you'd like to in 2011? Ready or not a new year is here. Put those 2011 things behind you and look with hope and confidence to this New Year.

One final thing; Tag you're it. You have been given a gift of a brand New Year. Don't be a hider be a seeker. Seek to make 2012 one of the best years you've ever had.

Roy is a national Conference, Seminar and Retreat speaker and can be contacted at Roy@royharris.info or view his website at www.royharris.info.

It's all in the details.

TABLES · CHAIRS
LINENS · NAPKINS
CHINA · GLASSWARE
FLATWARE · SILVER
WEDDING ACCESSORIES
CAKE ACCESSORIES
BRASS CANDELABRA
WROUGHT IRON CANDELABRA
& ACCESSORIES
SERVICE EQUIPMENT
CONFERENCE EQUIPMENT

Party Providers
YOUR SPECIAL EVENT RENTAL CENTER
(615) 443-3325
1012 WEST MAIN STREET · LEBANON

Tag, you're it!
By Roy W. Harris

Simon Says, raise your right hand! Red Rover Red Rover send Billy over! Simon Says and Red Rover are a couple of childhood games that we fondly remember playing especially with cousins. What in the world do kid games have to do with adult lives and the year 2012? Then there is that the other game called hide and seek. It was always more fun to be the hider rather than the seeker. Ready or not here I come were those key words that alerted all of us hiders that the seeker was on the way. Well, ready or not a New Year is not just on the way, it has already arrived. They seem to slip up on us sooner each year.

The book is now closed on 2011. But the good news is that 2012 brings with it great opportunities. You can close the chapters of failure and shortcomings of last year. That weight you wanted to lose, that project you wanted to start, those words you wish you'd said are all now in the past. It's almost like a chalk or marker board in school. When the teacher finishes one lesson he/she removes all evidence of it and moves on to the next.

2012 will add another volume to the books that make up our lives. The writing of it has already begun. It will contain multiple chapters with a variety of subjects; personal life, family relationships, work obligations, service to God and church and service to the community to name a few. There are some things

that might be wise for us to keep in mind. One way to do this is to ask ourselves a couple of questions:
What are some specific things I'd like to accomplish this coming year?

Many times things come up over and over again that we know need to be done. But somehow at the end of the year they still remain unfinished. Taking a few minutes in this first month of the year to jot down a to do list of things to be accomplished in 2012 can be a great way to organize your thoughts in a tangible way and will be a good starting point.

What is the most important thing I want to get done this year? Choosing the most important thing on the list is a great place to begin. Make it the top priority.

What should be the most important things on our lists for 2012? That's a great question! I believe we can never go wrong by remembering some principles designed to help guide us in determining the priorities of life. We have only to reflect upon the earliest form of spiritual guidelines, the Ten Commandments to find a successful model that has proven itself through the centuries. The summary of those commandments teaches us to place God first, others second and ourselves last.

What about ourselves? A man named Paul who penned a majority of the words in the New Testament of the Bible has some very good advice. He said something like this: I haven't accomplished all I'd like to yet, but I've put the past behind me and I'm looking ahead to the future. I've set a goal and now I'm working to accomplish it. I have confidence that I

will succeed in the end (Philippians 4:13-14). This is great advice for us today. So what if you didn't accomplish all you'd like to in 2011? Ready or not a new year is here. Put those 2011 things behind you and look with hope and confidence to this New Year.
One final thing; Tag you're it. You have been given a gift of a brand New Year. Don't be a hider be a seeker. Seek to make 2012 one of the best years you've ever had.

Roy is a national Conference, Seminar and Retreat speaker and can be contacted at **roy@royharris.** info or view his website at www.royharris.info.

OUT OF AFRICA

Roy's wife, Arly, showing the locals an American "high five."

Roy and one of his fellow pastors.

By ROY HARRIS

When you hear the word Africa, what comes to mind? No doubt things like lions, leopards, elephants and perhaps giraffes. Maybe the book by Karen von Bixen called *Out of Africa* which inspired the movie by the same name.

All of those things come to mind for me and so much more. I am honored and very blessed to have opportunities to speak in most of our states here in America and also a number of countries around the globe. I had the unique opportunity a couple of months ago to travel to East Africa to the country of Kenya. I was the keynote speaker at a pastors' conference for 350 church leaders from Kenya, Uganda, Burundi and Rwanda. What a wonderful experience it was and one I will never forget.

My 24-hour flight from Nashville featured stops in Detroit, Amsterdam and finally arriving in Nairobi the capital of Kenya, the largest city in East Africa. A

Out of Africa

By
Dr. Roy W. Harris

When you hear the word Africa, what comes to mind? No doubt things like lions, leopards, elephants and perhaps giraffes. Maybe the book by Karen von Blixen called *Out of Africa,* *which* inspired the movie by the same name. All of those things come to mind for me and so much more. I am honored and very blessed to have opportunities to speak in most of our states here in America and also a number of countries around the globe. I had the unique opportunity a couple of months ago to travel to East Africa to the country of Kenya. I was the keynote speaker at a pastors' conference for 350 church leaders from Kenya, Uganda, Burundi and Rwanda. What a wonderful experience it was and one I will never forget.

My twenty-four hour flight from Nashville featured stops in Detroit, Amsterdam and finally arriving in in Nairobi the capital of Kenya, the largest city in East Africa. A smaller plane then delivered me safely to the city of Eldoret 200 miles northwest near the Ugandan border.

Not sure what to expect, I exited the baggage claim area and walked into the main terminal. Three well-dressed tall African men greeted me with the traditional African greeting of three embraces each. Two elementary age girls, dressed in bright red dresses and hair filled with braids and beads, formally welcomed to Kenya presenting me with a small Kenyan flag and my Official Speaker's Badge for the week. We loaded up and headed for my hotel. The headlights on our van illuminated the surrounding countryside and this Tennessee boy knew he was not in Tennessee anymore. This began a week I will never forget.

There is an eight-hour time difference between Tennessee and Kenya but I came to realize there is also *U.S. Time & African Time* in a different sense. Nine-o-clock in the morning U.S. Time could mean nine-fifteen, nine-thirty or nine-forty five African Time. When I arrived for the first session of the conference, I also soon came to realize that running water and electricity were not the norm for most people attending this conference. Only one person owned a car and most had walked, ridden bicycles or traveled up to two days by bus to get to the conference. The conference was held in a huge tent in a fenced field complete with sheep, goats and chickens moving freely outside the tent. A portable generator supplied power to operate the sound system.

The African people were a joy to be with. I was impressed immediately with their smiling faces and friendly dispositions. They were neatly dressed. The ladies wore bright colored clothing and many of the men wore coats and ties. Many of ladies made their multi-colored clothing for them and their children. I was also impressed with how gifted and talented they were. Most of them were tri-lingual speaking English, their individual Tribal languages and Swahili the most common language of Africa. They played a variety of instruments and had beautiful voices. They loved to sing and incorporated native African dance into each song.

The Conference began on Monday morning and was completed on Thursday afternoon with presentation of certificates to those who'd attended all four days.

My wife Amy and her mother Diane were able to join me earlier in the week and Friday began a new chapter in our Kenya experience. We left Eldoret early on Friday morning to visit some very special people about fifty miles away near Katali, Kenya. We had the privilege of visiting three orphanages and a Bible Institute that trains bi-vocational pastors. Our first stop introduced us to an orphanage school, which cared for and taught about 100 children. We were amazed at how well behaved the children were and how much the teachers were able to do with very limited resources. They taught the basics using poster board taped to the walls. We asked the children if there was anything they wished they had for school. One little boy said: "our soccer ball was destroyed by a storm; could we get a new one?" The school could not afford a new one (we made sure they got a new one). This was typical of what we found in all three of the orphanage schools.

I was involved with Christian Education for almost twenty-five years so having the opportunity to visit and speak in educational settings to children and young adults was near to my heart. The Bible Institute semester had ended a couple of weeks earlier but several students made a special trip back to campus to hear me speak. I couldn't help but notice the surroundings. No running water. No indoor plumbing. No electricity. The sky could be seen through small holes in the tin roof. I encouraged those special students to pursue excellence and finish their education.

What did I bring back *Out of Africa*?

I am always thankful for America each time I return from overseas. I was even more thankful upon returning from Africa for the basic things we enjoy and take for granted. Things like; using tap water instead of bottled water to brush my teeth, having hot water instead of cold to shave and shower with, having our own vehicles with the ability to drive anywhere we would choose to go, having electricity and all the benefits and appliances which go with it, having homes with closeable windows and floors made of materials other than clay or mud, having plenty of food and grocery stores to buy more. I'm thankful for being able to spend nights in hotels without armed guards in a compound like setting. I'm thankful for houses of worship where we have actual buildings with carpet, padded seats or pews, central heat and air, indoor plumbing, electricity complete with lights so activities can also take place after sunset rather than tents which have none of these.

I also brought back from Africa a great appreciation for the African people. They are industrious, happy and joyful people. The African Christians have a great love for Christ and their religion. Although they live on very meager resources, they sacrificially give to help the needs of others. They are gifted people who are excellent craftsmen and talented musicians and singers.

I've accepted an invitation to return to Africa again this fall for a second time. I'll be speaking at a citywide crusade along with training hundreds of church leaders during three days of pastors' conference sessions. I may be physically Out of Africa now, but a part of me will always be with the African people. I'm reminded of the scriptures' admonition; *to whom much is given much will be required.* We have been given much in America. We really cannot appreciation how much until we visit those who have so much less. With this great gift comes great responsibility. Out of America has always flowed generosity to help the world. I feel fortunate and so blessed to be an American. I know you probably feel the same. If you have any doubt, just talk to someone fresh Out of Africa.

Books In Print

Common Sense Leadership

by Dr Roy W Harris

MINISTERING in East AFRICA
A Common Sense APPROACH

Dr. Roy W. Harris

Kusaidia Kwa Familia

Daktari
Roy W. Harris

LEAD WITH CONFIDENCE
Using Common Sense

Dr. Roy Harris

MALEZI YALIYO NA HIZIA NJEMA

Dr. Roy W. Harris

Anthony Lusichi Mbukhitsa

Dr. Roy W. Harris'
Doctoral Dissertation

Exploration of
Caregiver Transition

Roy Harris